Mel Bay's
FUN WITH THE
MELODY FLUTE

By Mizzy McCaskill
& Dona Gilliam

A cassette tape of the music in this book is now available. The publisher strongly recommends the use of this cassette tape along with the text to insure accuracy of interpretation and ease in learning.

Contents

Preface

The melody flute is a member of the fipple flute family. Beginners find melody flutes much easier to play than traditional side-blown flutes due to the fipple mouthpiece encircling the embouchure hole (blow hole). The fipple windway channels the player's airstream into and over the tube and allows the creation of sound by blowing into the mouthpiece. This simplicity of tone production makes the melody flute an ideal first instrument for the beginning flute or fife player.

The melody flute is pitched in the key of 'C' and sounds the fundamental pitch of 'C' when all of the tone holes are covered. A 'C' Major scale can be played by lifting one finger at a time (see fingering chart). Players wishing to advance to the fife or tin whistle will be able to adapt quickly as this fingering pattern is common to both instruments. Easy and versatile, the melody flute will provide the beginning player with instant musical success and hours of enjoyment.

Melody Flute Fingering Chart

○ open hole
● closed hole

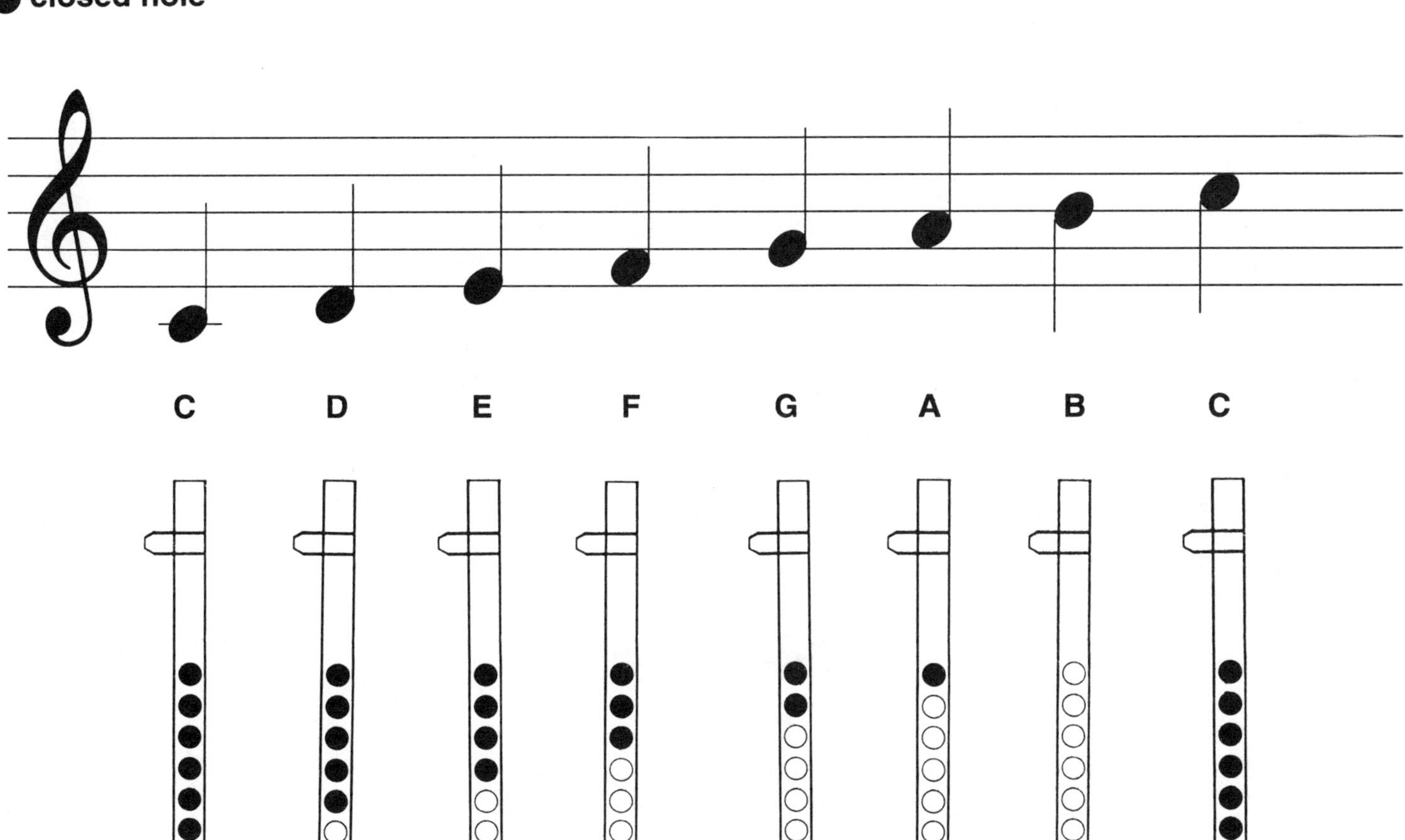

Musical Facts

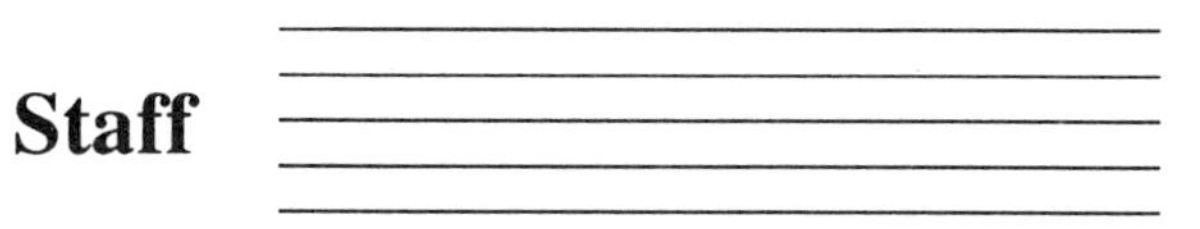

Staff

Treble Clef

The **staff** consists of five lines and four **spaces** upon which notes are placed.

A **treble clef** or **G-clef** is placed at the beginning of a staff. It indicates the pitch of the notes to follow because it circles the **G** line.

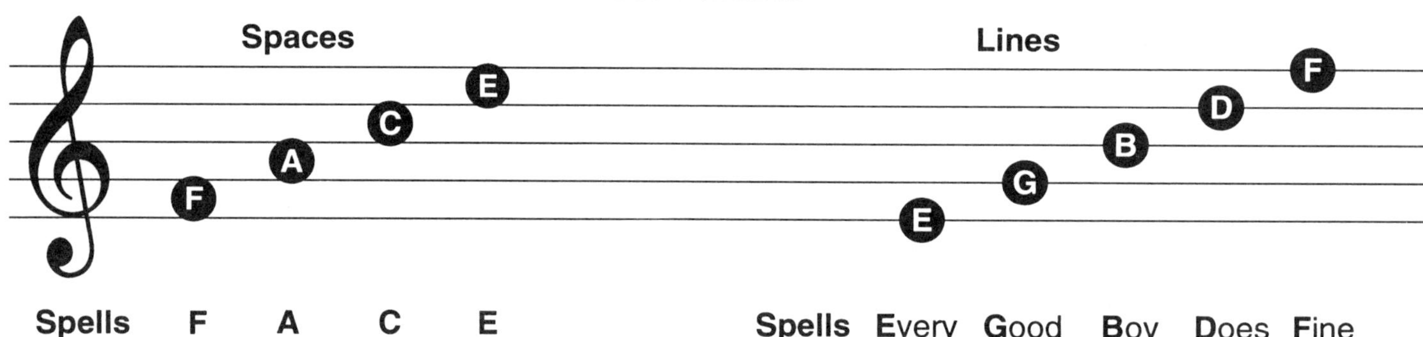

Bar lines are used to divide the staff into measures.
The space between two bar lines is called a **measure.**
The **double bar line** is used at the end of a musical selection.

Note Names

Spells   F   A   C   E   Spells   Every   Good   Boy   Does   Fine

Note and Rest Values

Whole Note

Half Notes

Quarter Notes

Count   1   2   3   4

Whole Rest

Half Rests

Quarter Rests

Count   1   2   3   4

Time Signature

4   3   2   Top number tells how many counts in a measure
4,   4,   4   Bottom number tells what kind of note recieves
              one count (, or quarter note)

Playing Position

To Hold:

Cover the **top** three tone holes with the first three fingers of the **left** hand.

Cover the **bottom** three tone holes with the first three fingers of the **right** hand.

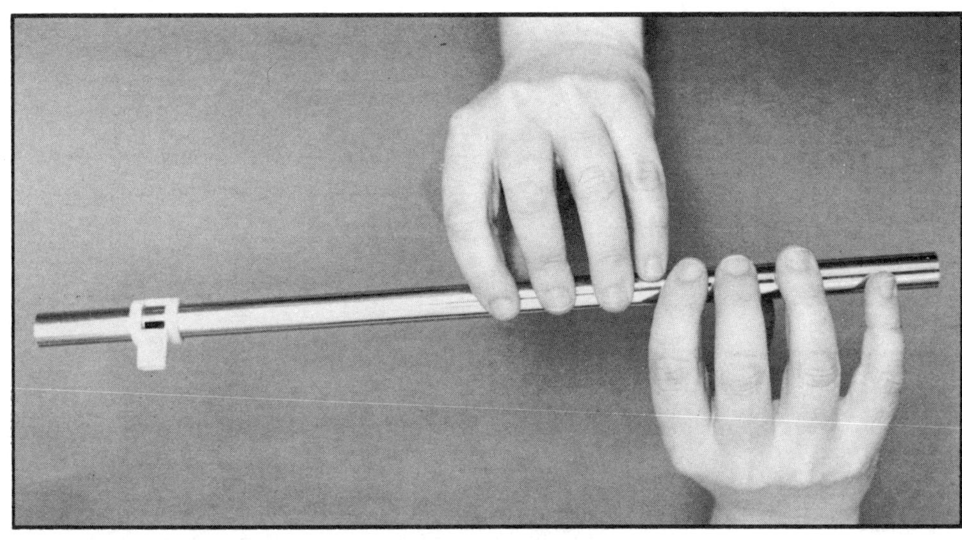

Question: Why place the left hand on top of the flute and the right hand on the bottom of the flute? Why not reverse the hands?

Answer: If you advance to the recorder, flute, saxophone, clarinet, oboe, or bassoon you will already have proper playing position.

To Sound:

Sit up straight. Place the mouthpiece between the lips. Instrument rests on thumbs. Take a normal breath, and move tongue as if saying 'too' while blowing a steady stream of air.

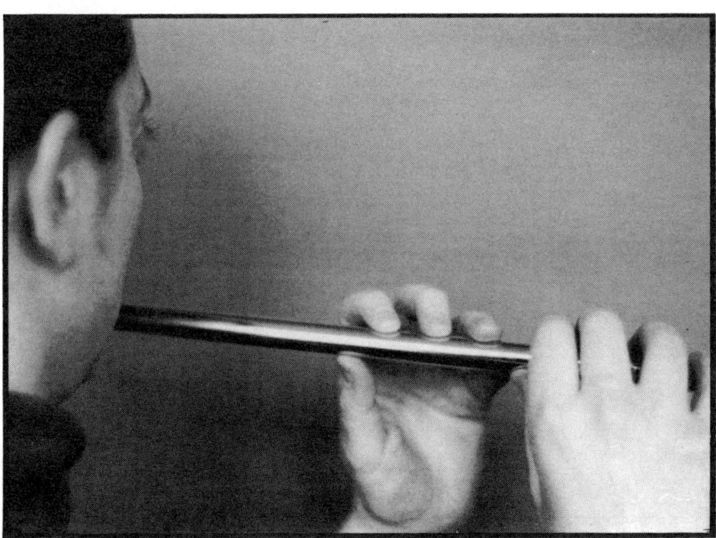

Photographs by Dawn M. Terminella

First Notes B, A, and G

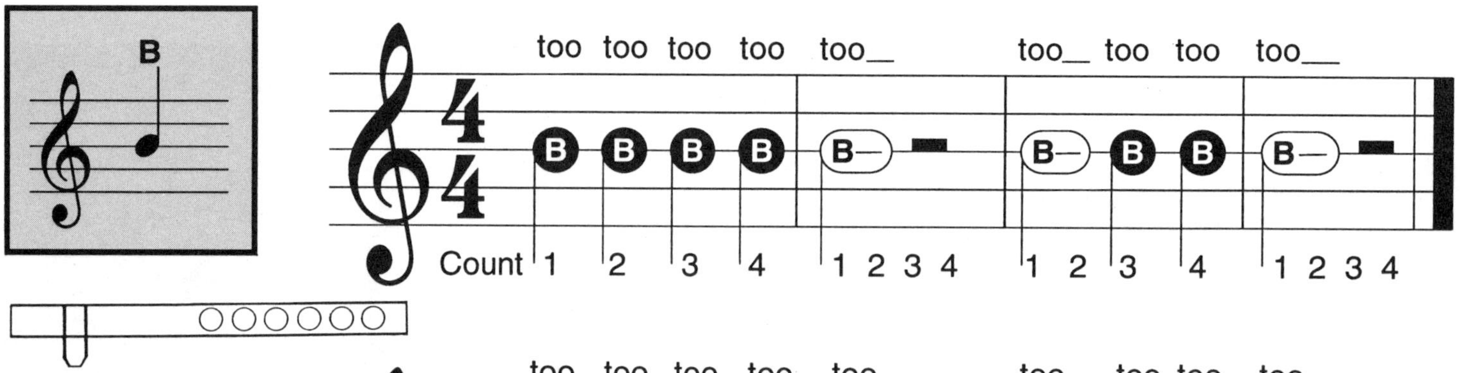

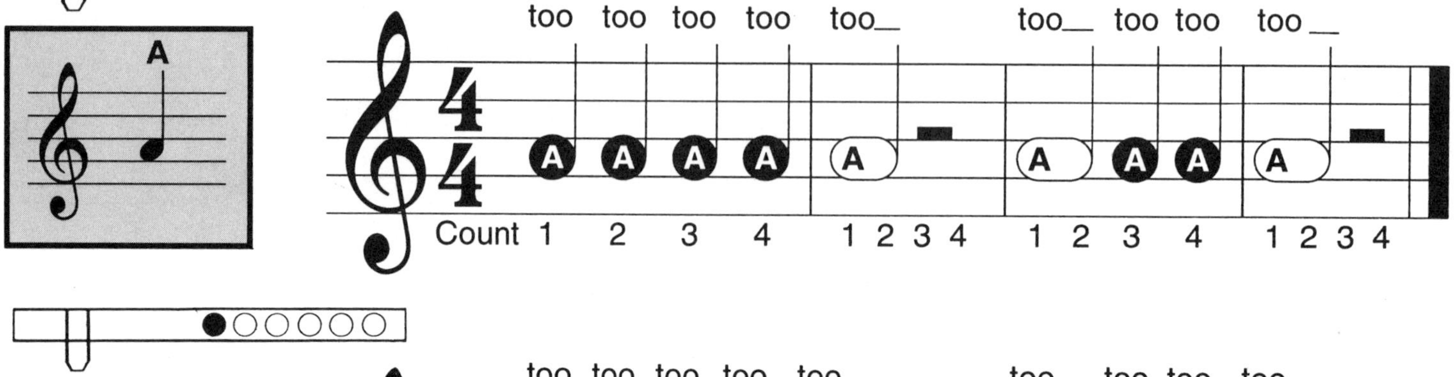

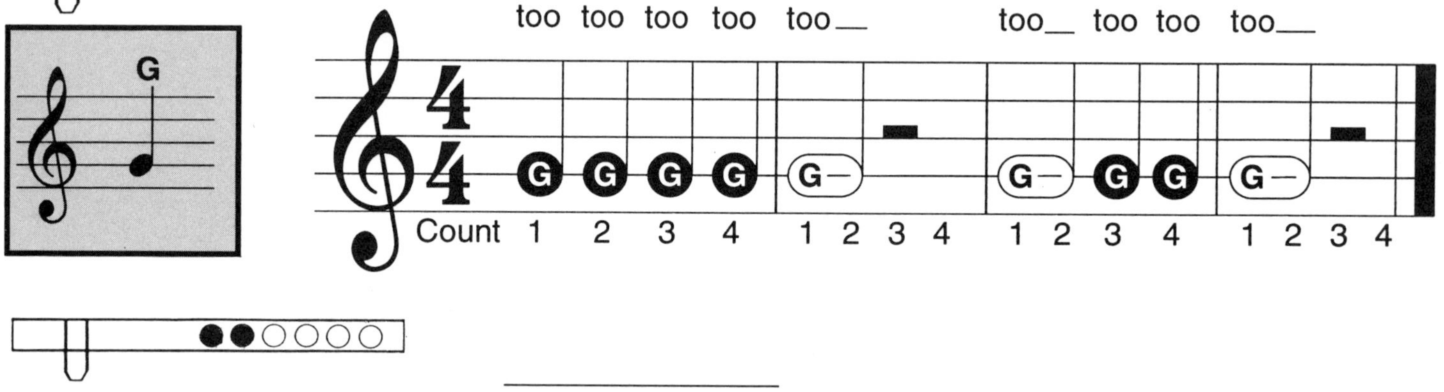

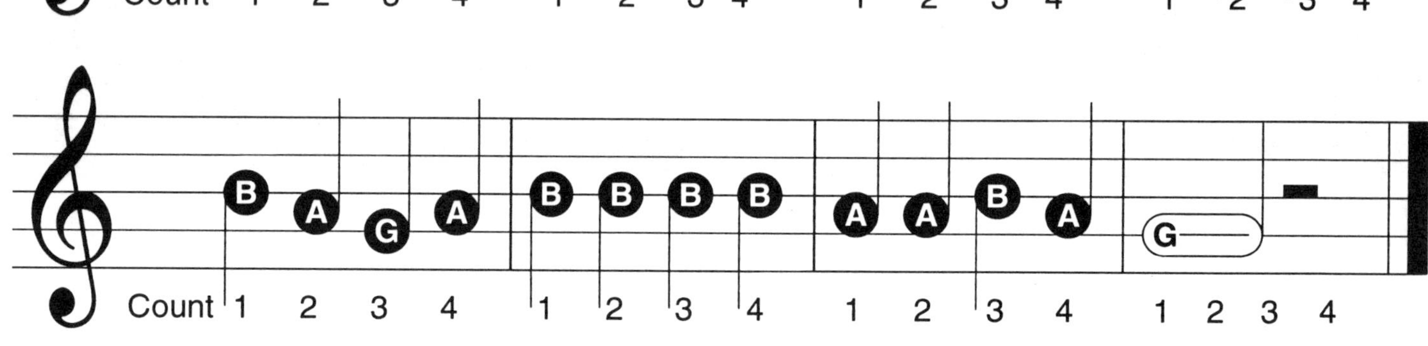

Half Rest  — The **half rest** receives two counts. Notice that it sits on a line.

Merrily We Roll Along

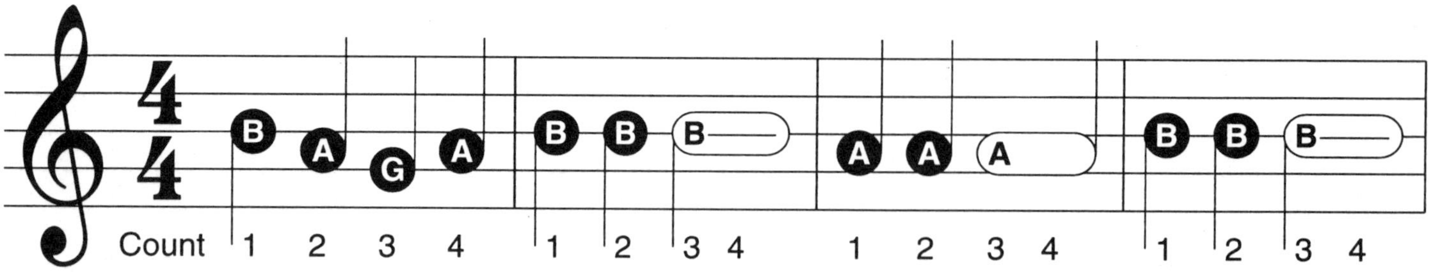

Hot Cross Buns

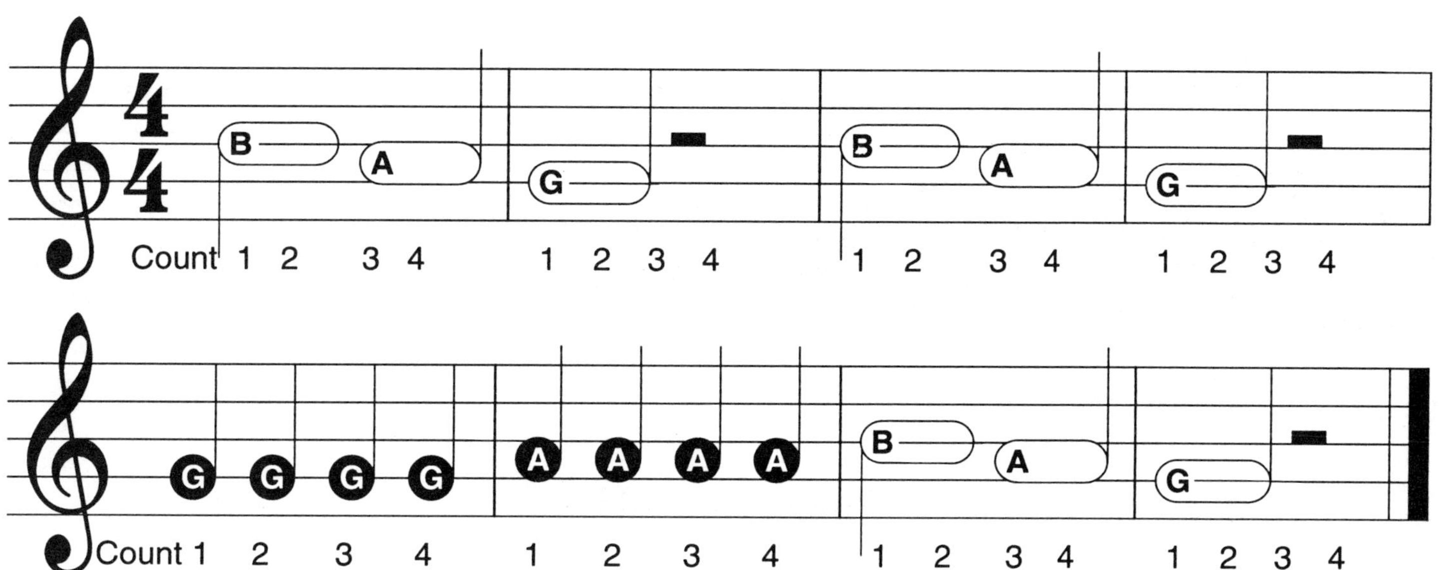

Repeat Signs 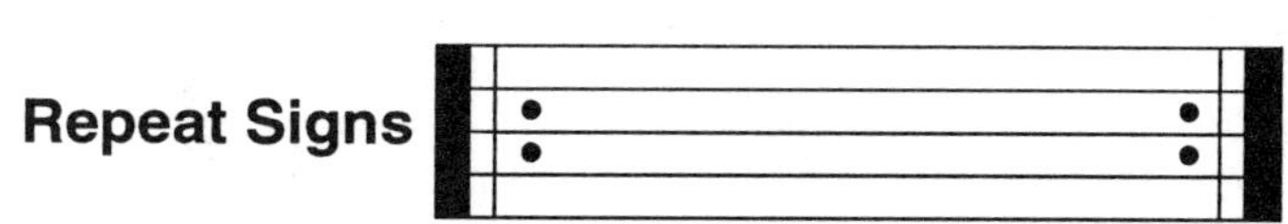

Repeat signs indicate that music between the two signs is to be repeated. If only one repeat sign is used return to the beginning.

Au Clair de la Lune

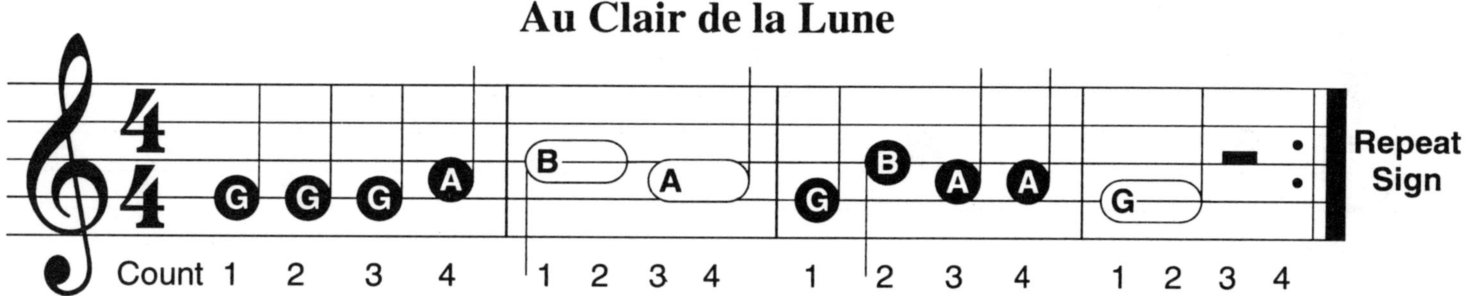

Quarter Rest 

The **quarter rest** receives one count.

Fais Do Do

New Note F

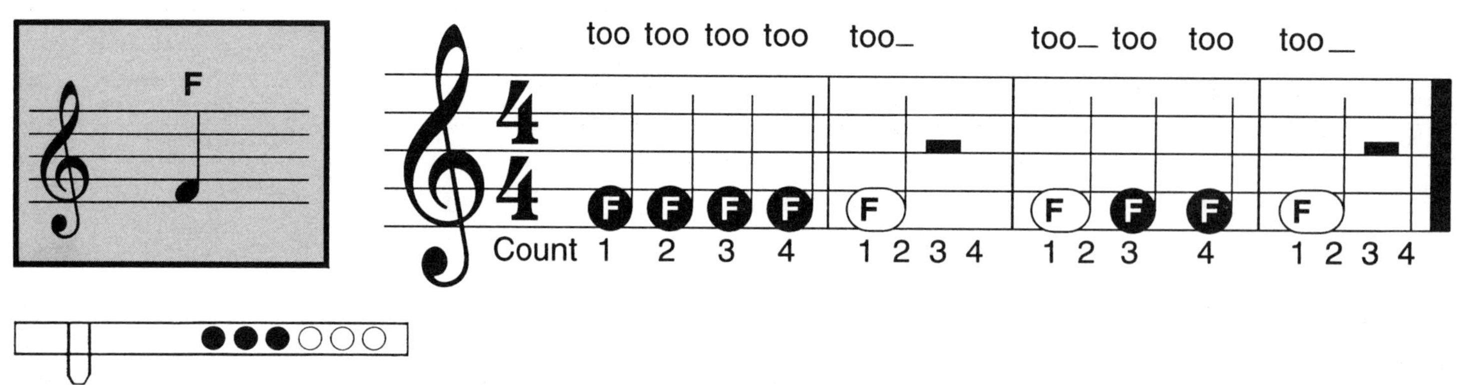

Fingering Guide

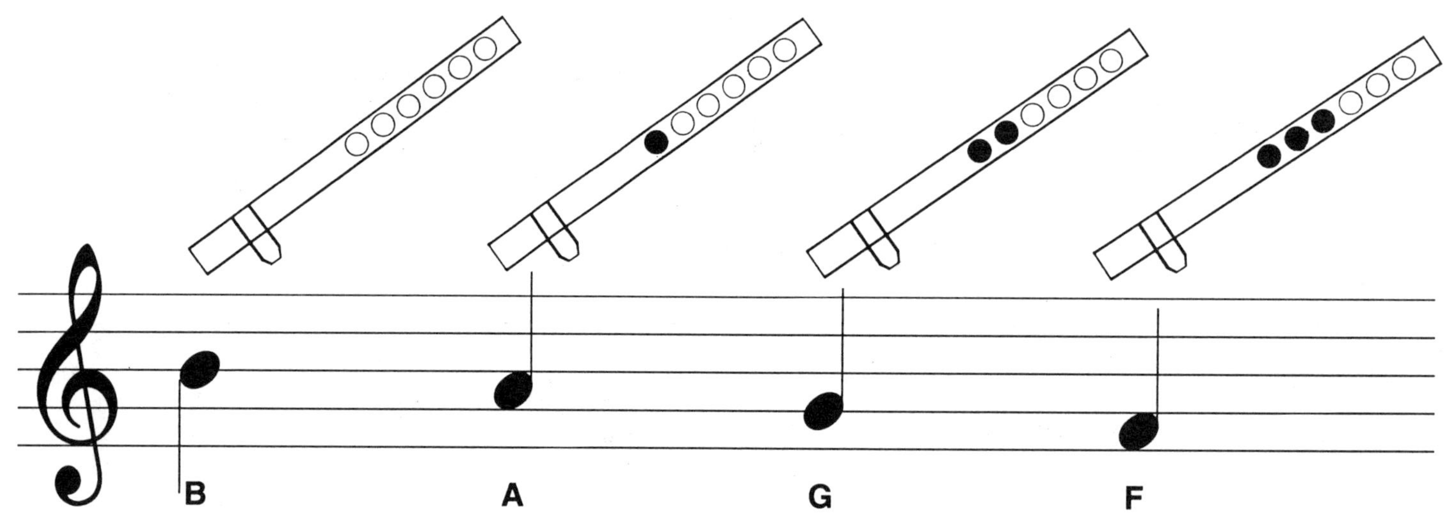

Merrily We Roll Along

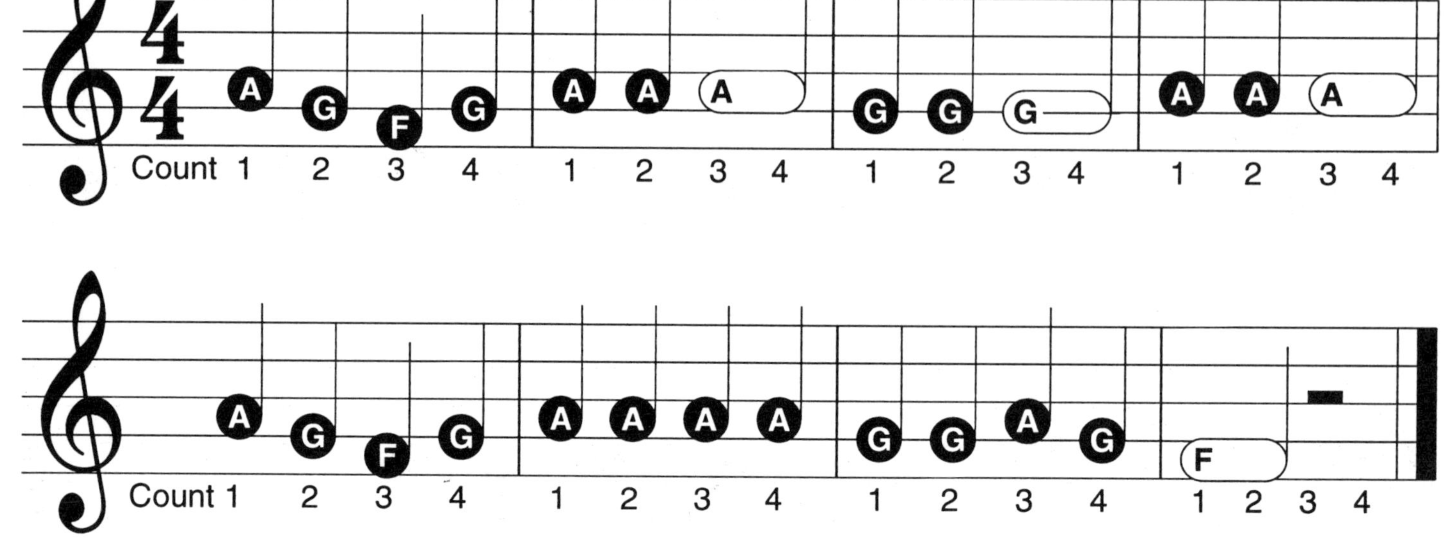

Au Clair de la Lune

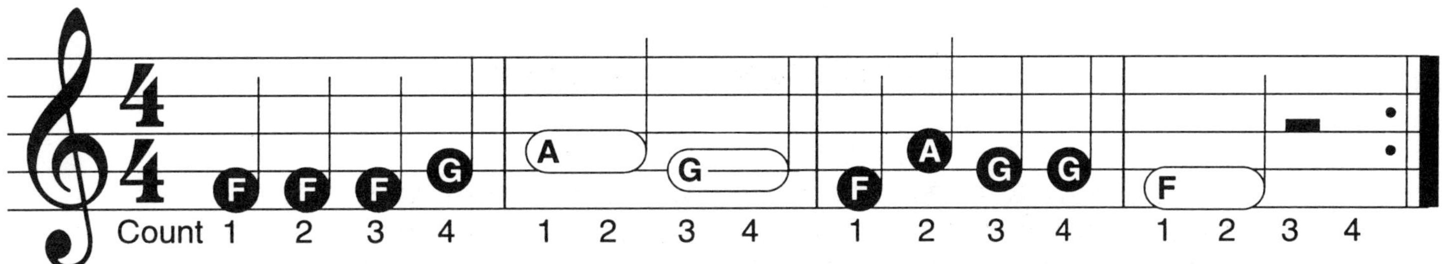

Hot Cross Buns

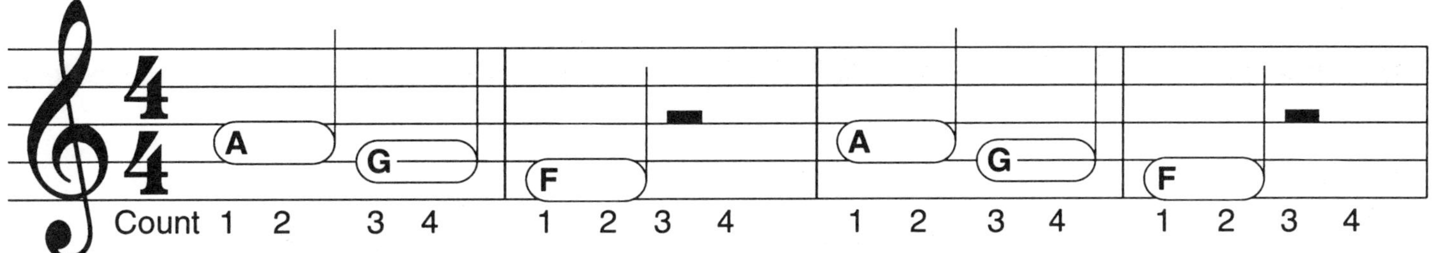

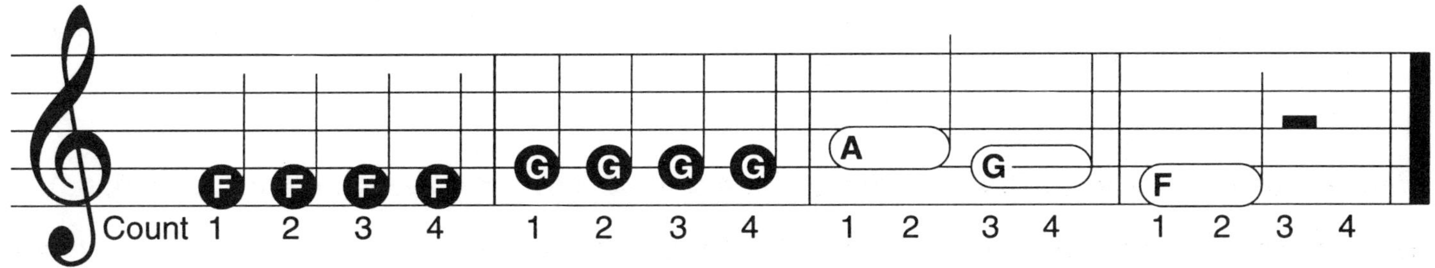

Fais Do Do

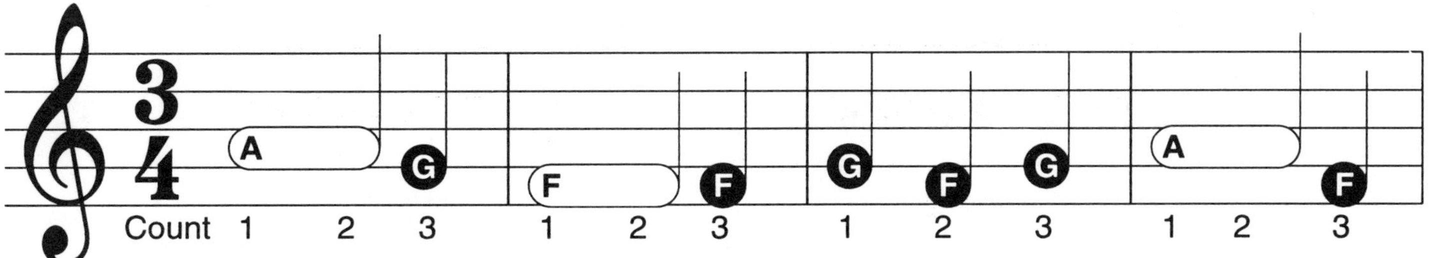

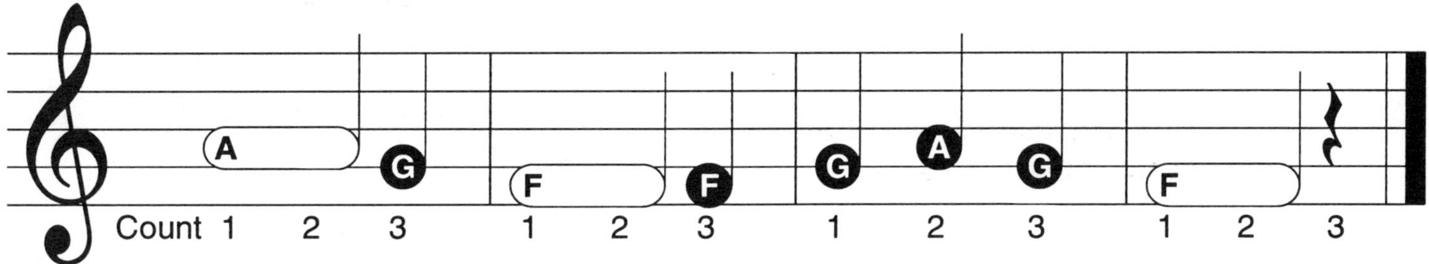

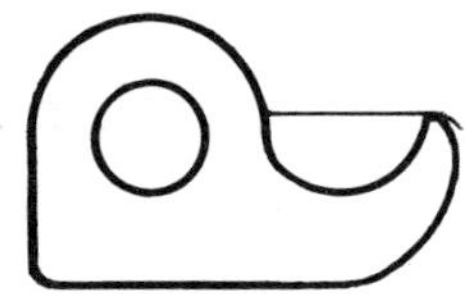

Use of Taped Tone Holes

The following pages recommend the use of **transparent tape** when practicing the lowest notes on the melody flute. The tape is used to cover the tone holes and to assist the player in establishing correct pitch and playing position. Players who are able to control closure of all tone holes may choose not to use the tape. When tape is not used, simply follow the open (o) or closed (●) fingerings as given.

Tape 6 Holes

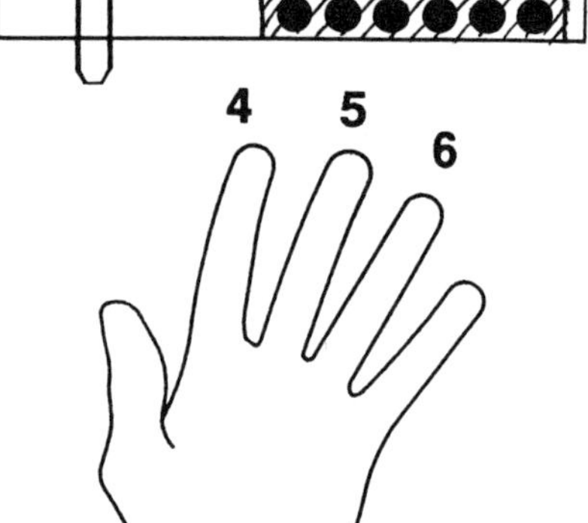

Make sure tape seals all six tone holes.

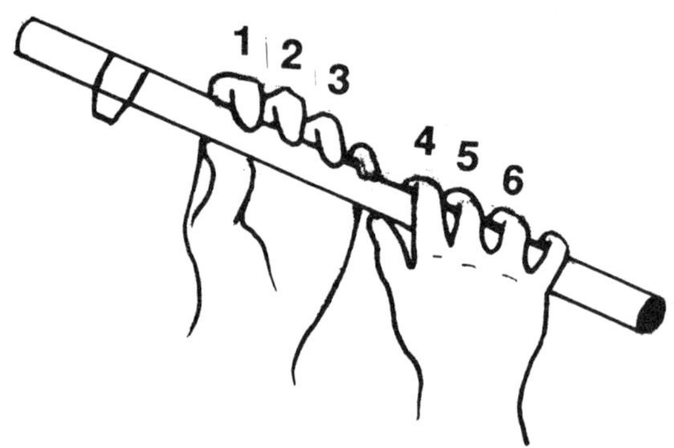

Place fingers **1, 2,** and **3** of the **left** hand on the **top** three tone holes (over the transparent tape).

Place fingers **4, 5,** and **6** of the **right** hand on the **bottom** three tone holes (over the transparent tape).

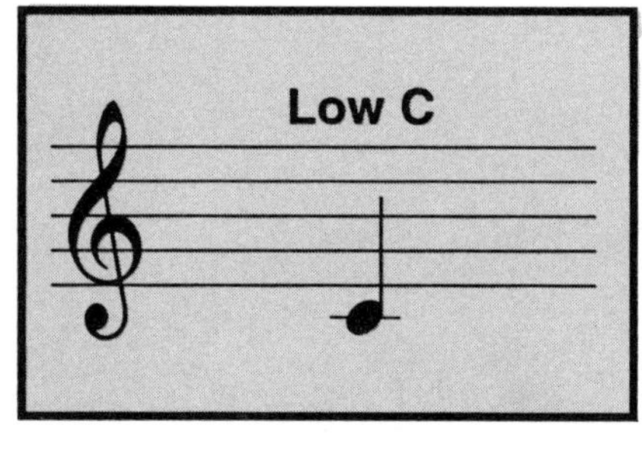

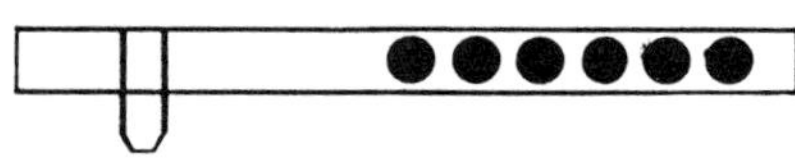

Blow very **softly.**
Play a **low** note.

Blow a **fast** air stream.
Play a **high** note.

How long can you hold **Low C**?
Count the seconds.

How long can you hold **High C**?
Count the seconds.

Octave Exercises

The same fingering produces a low or high note depending upon the speed of the air stream. Low C and High C are one **Octave** apart.

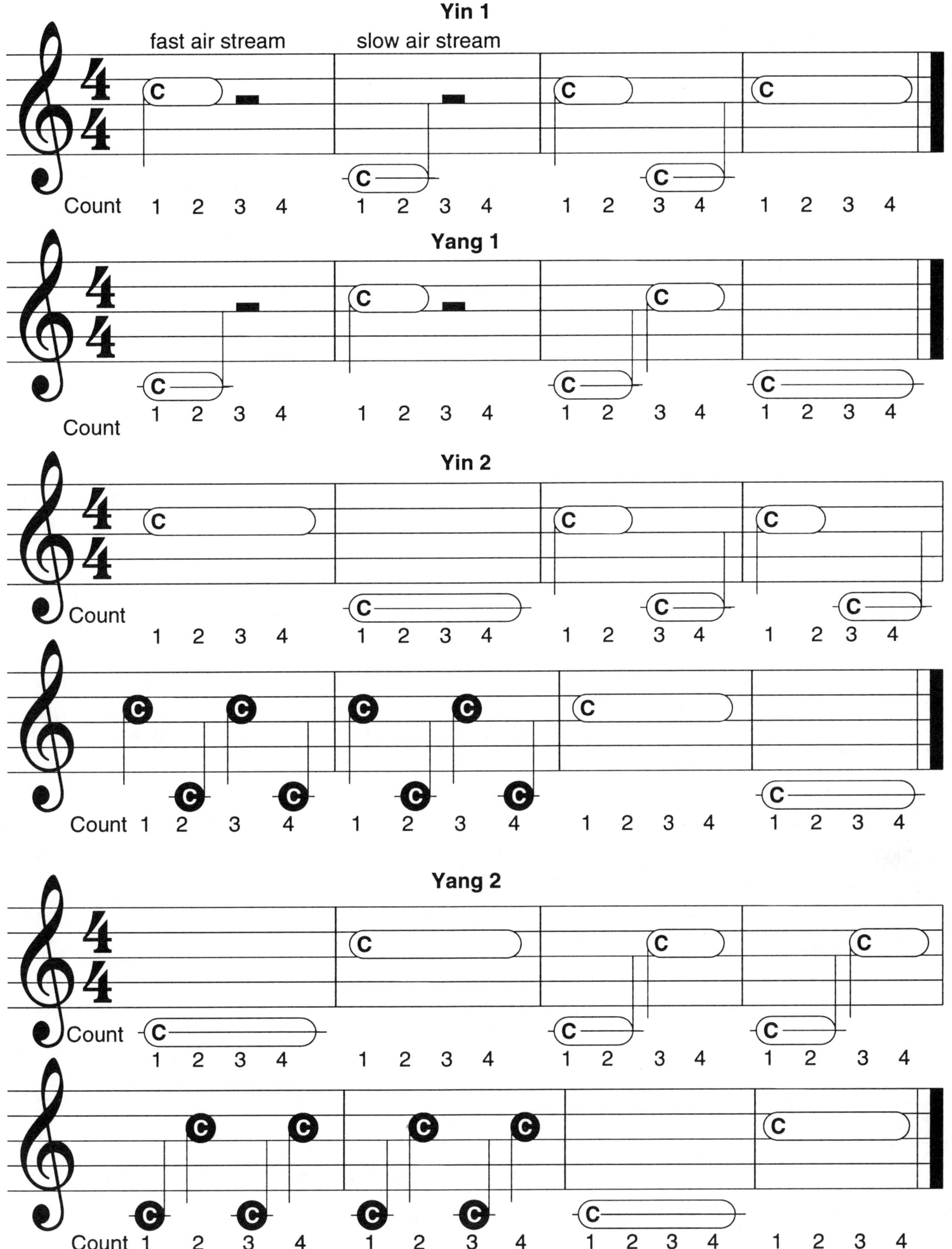

New Notes D and E

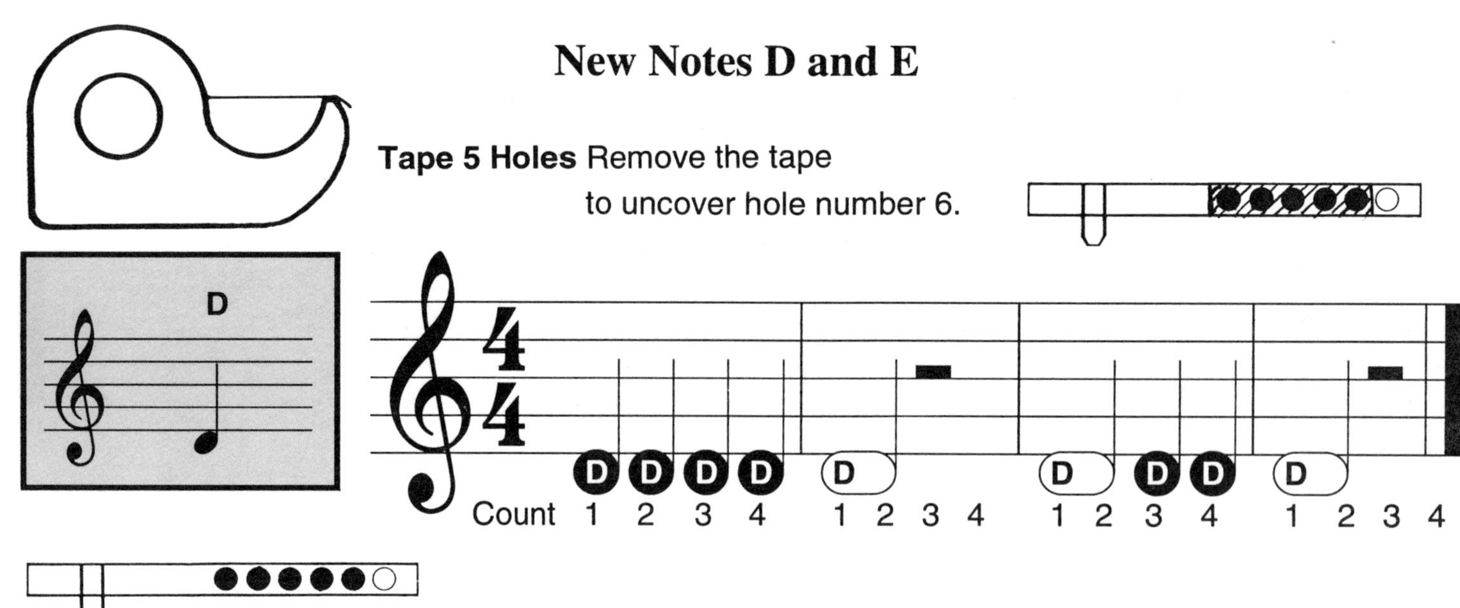

Finger Exercise

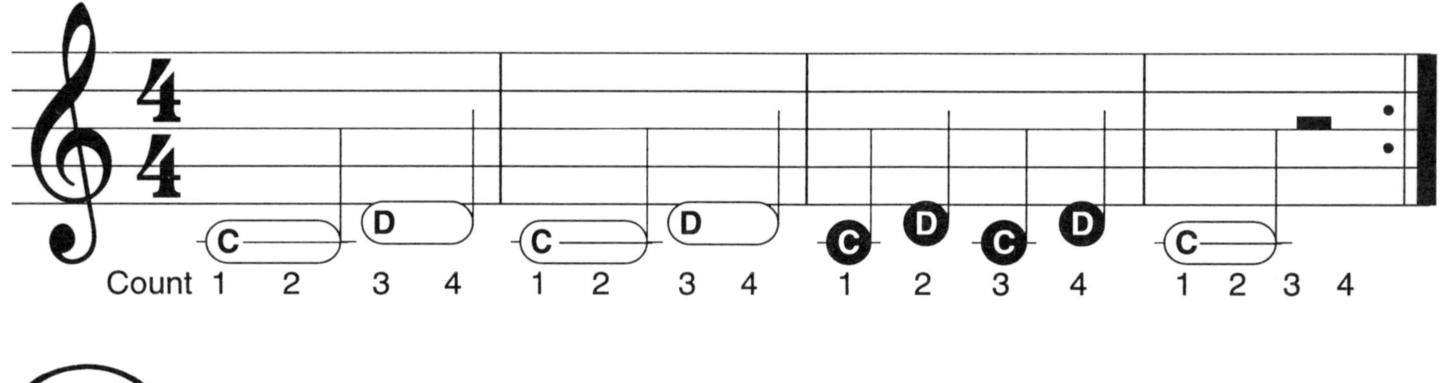

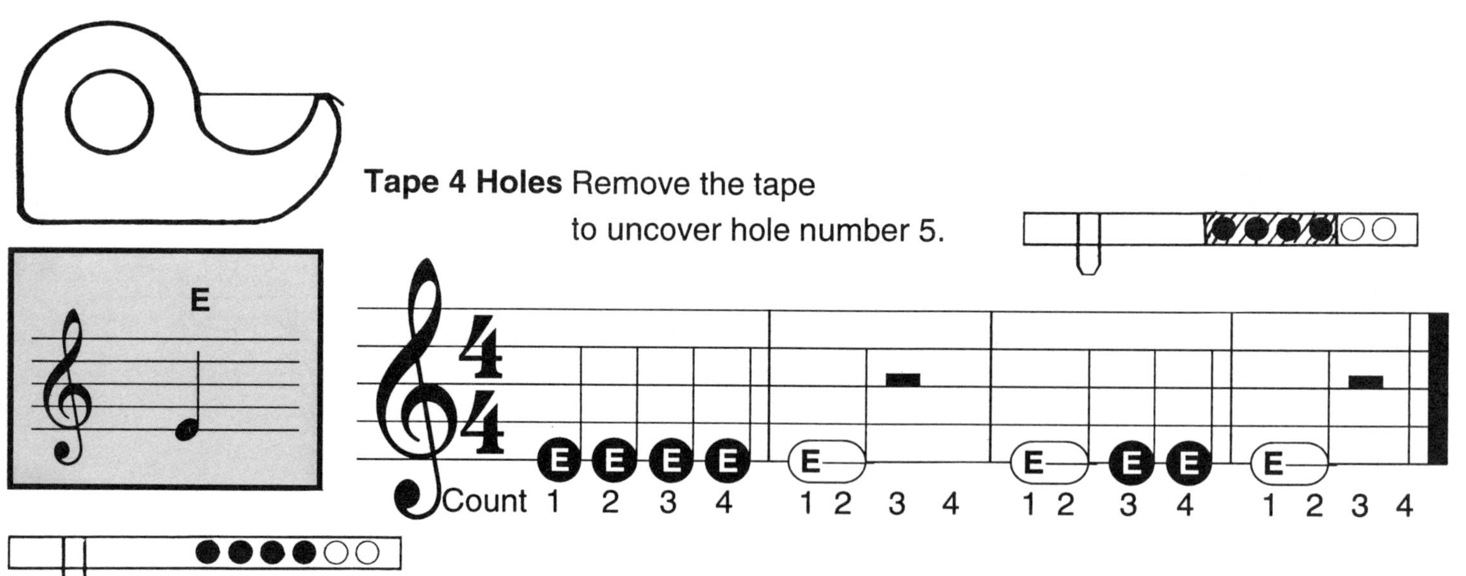

Finger Exercise

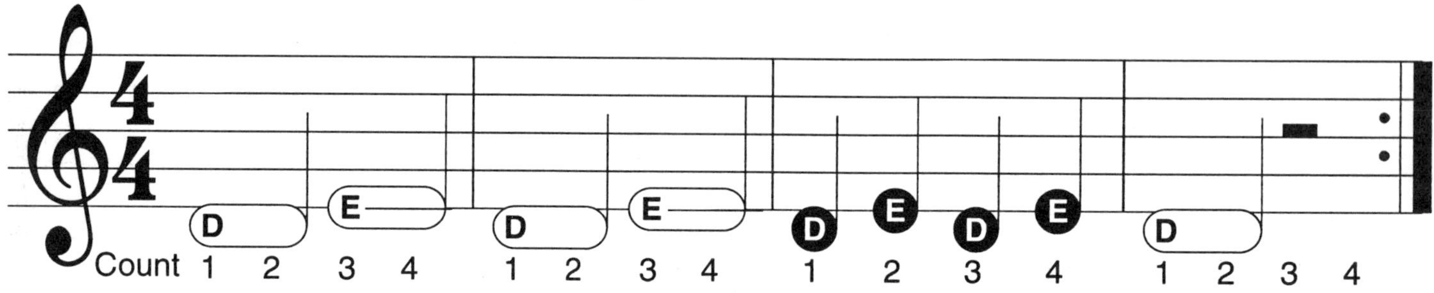

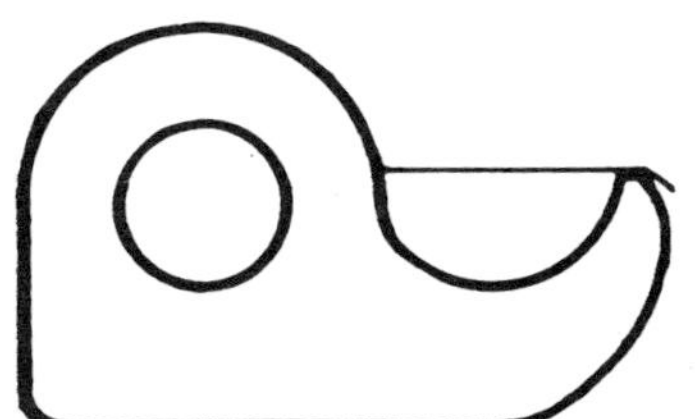

Tape 3 Holes Remove the tape to uncover hole number 4.

Finger Exercise

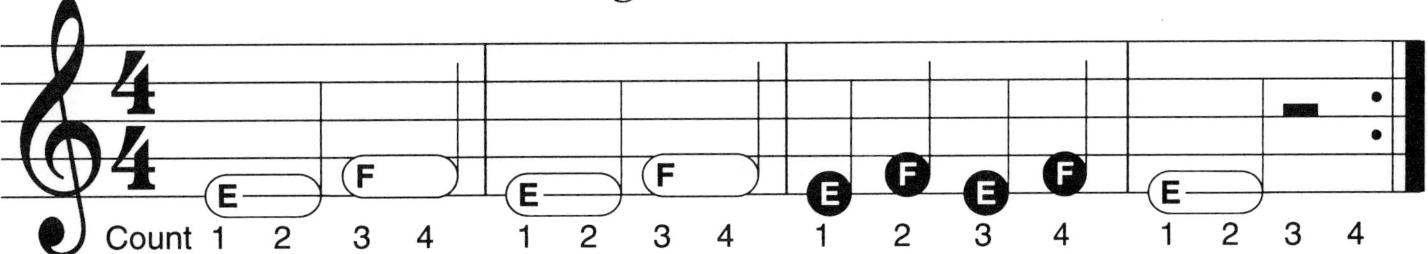

Whole Rest

The **whole rest** receives four counts. Notice that it hangs from the line.

Whole Rest Exercise

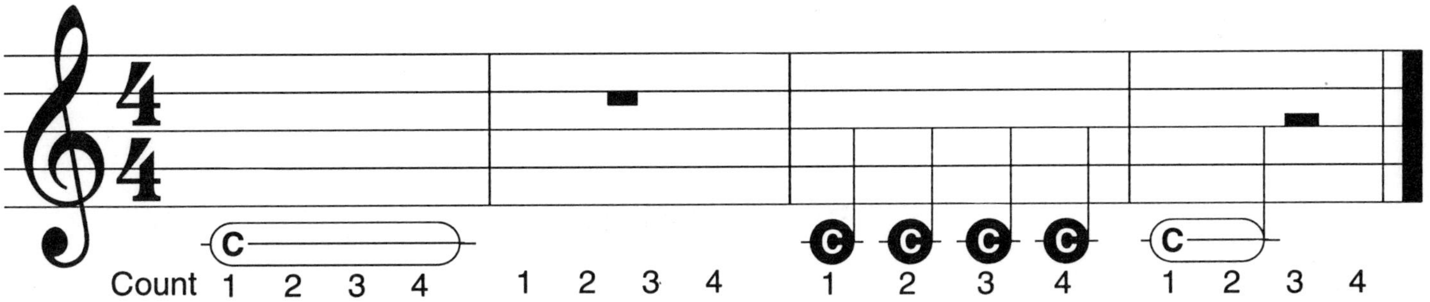

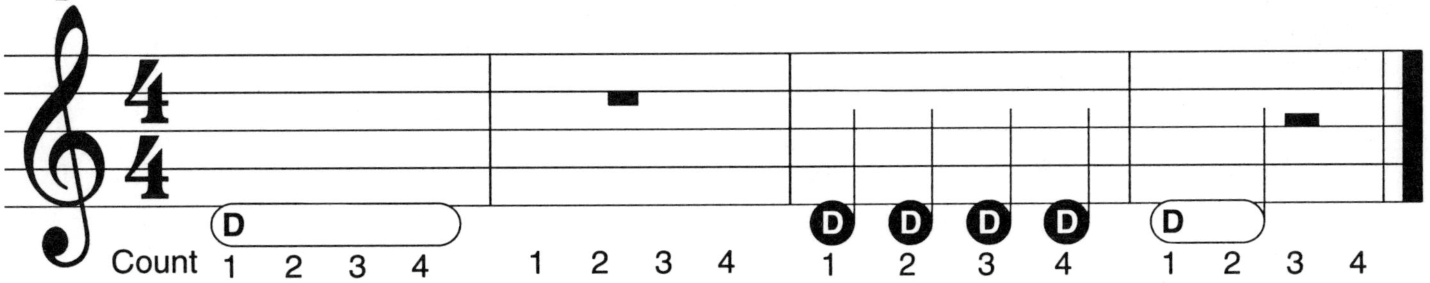

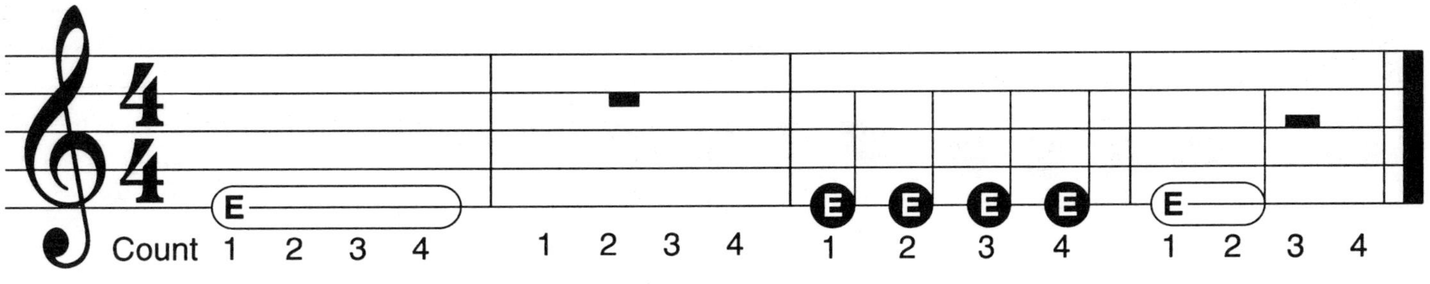

Points to Remember:

1. Tongue the beginning of each note as if saying 'too'.

2. Blow a slow, steady air stream.

3. Should moisture form in the mouthpiece and prevent notes from sounding, remove moisture by placing finger over the fipple and blowing hard.

Fingering Guide

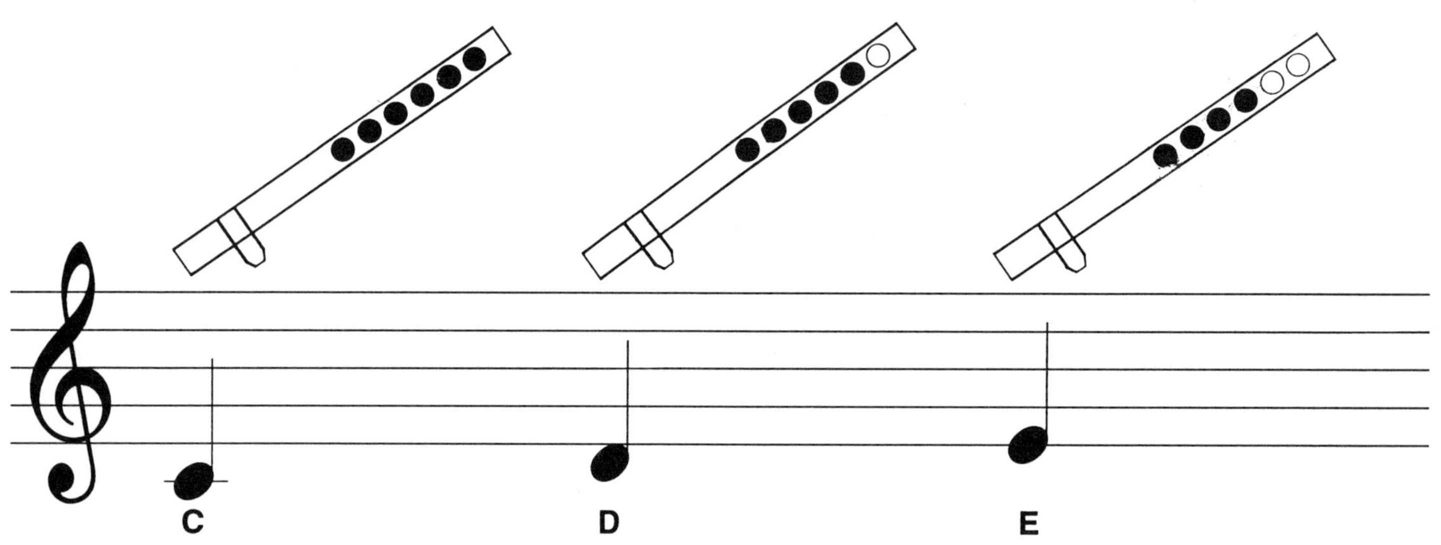

Hot Cross Buns

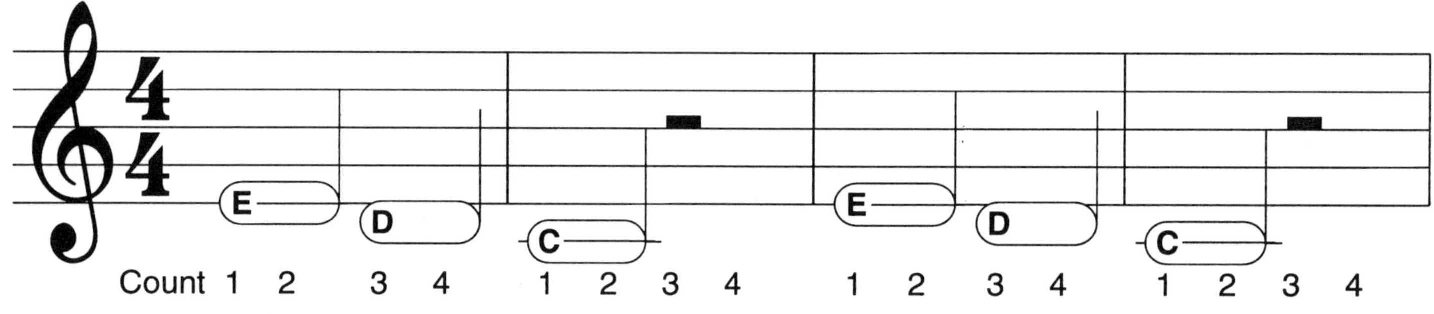

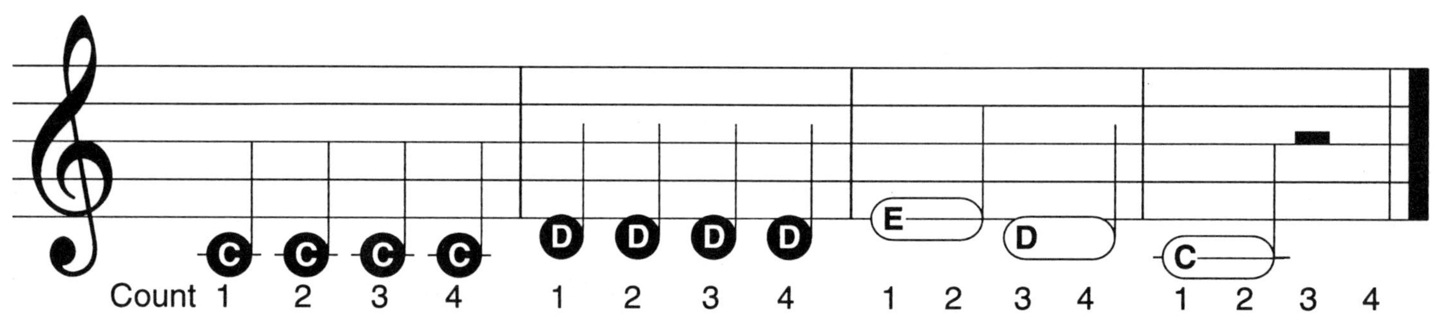

Au Clair de la Lune

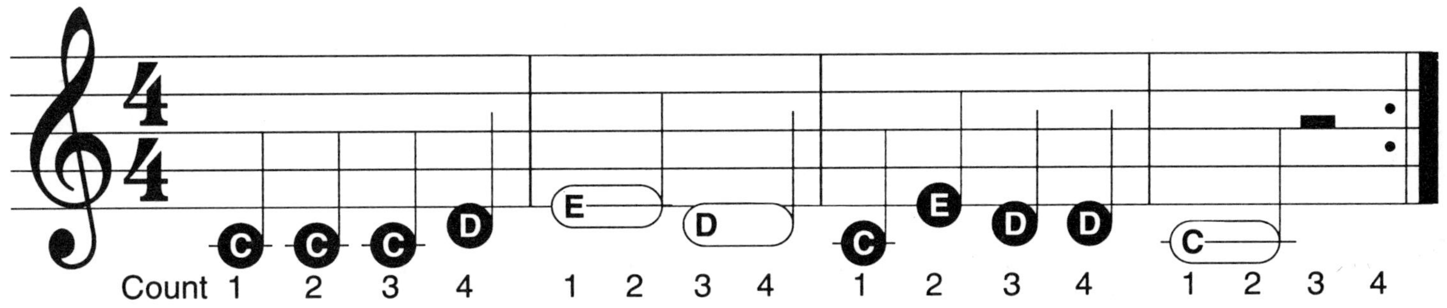

Merrily We Roll Along

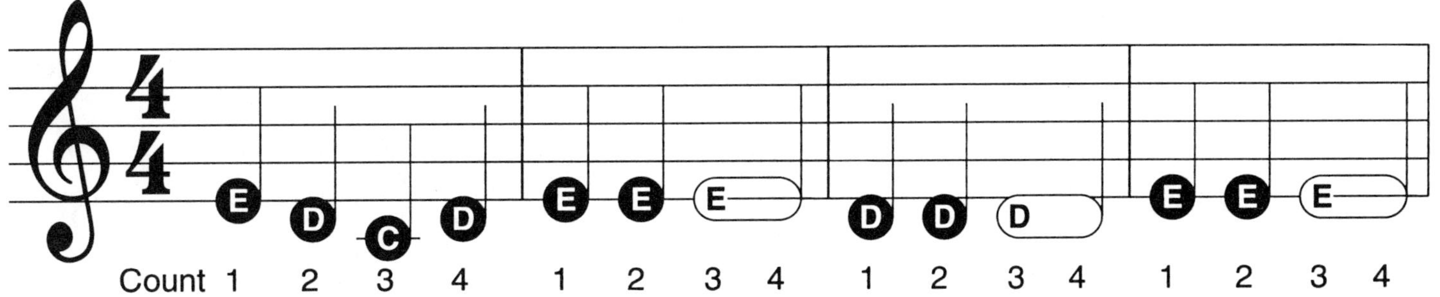

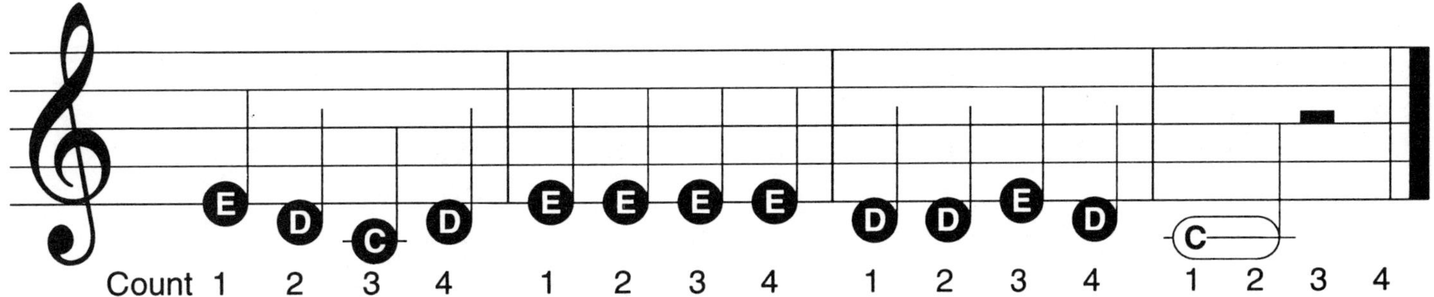

Fais Do Do

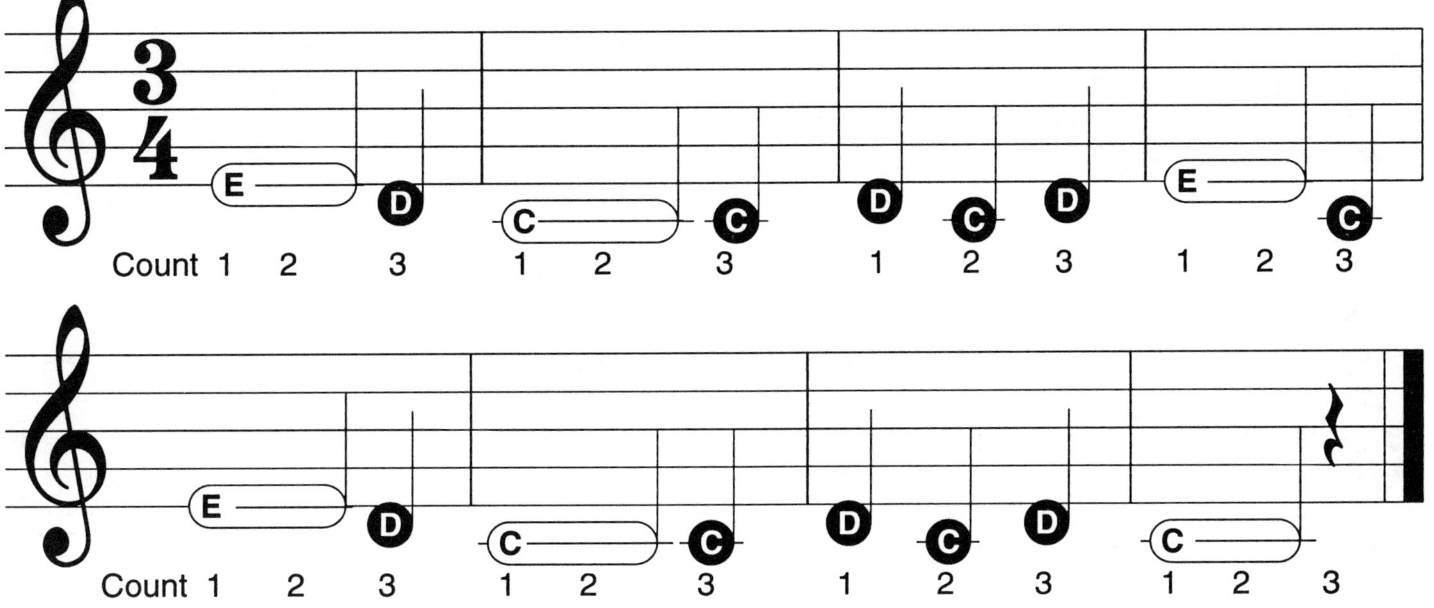

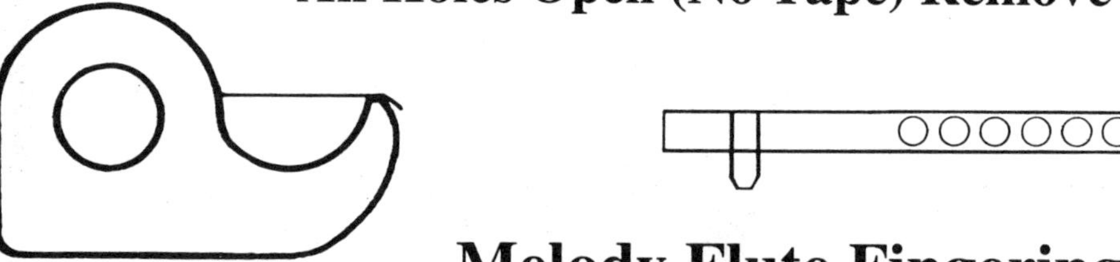

Melody Flute Fingering Chart

○ open hole
● closed hole

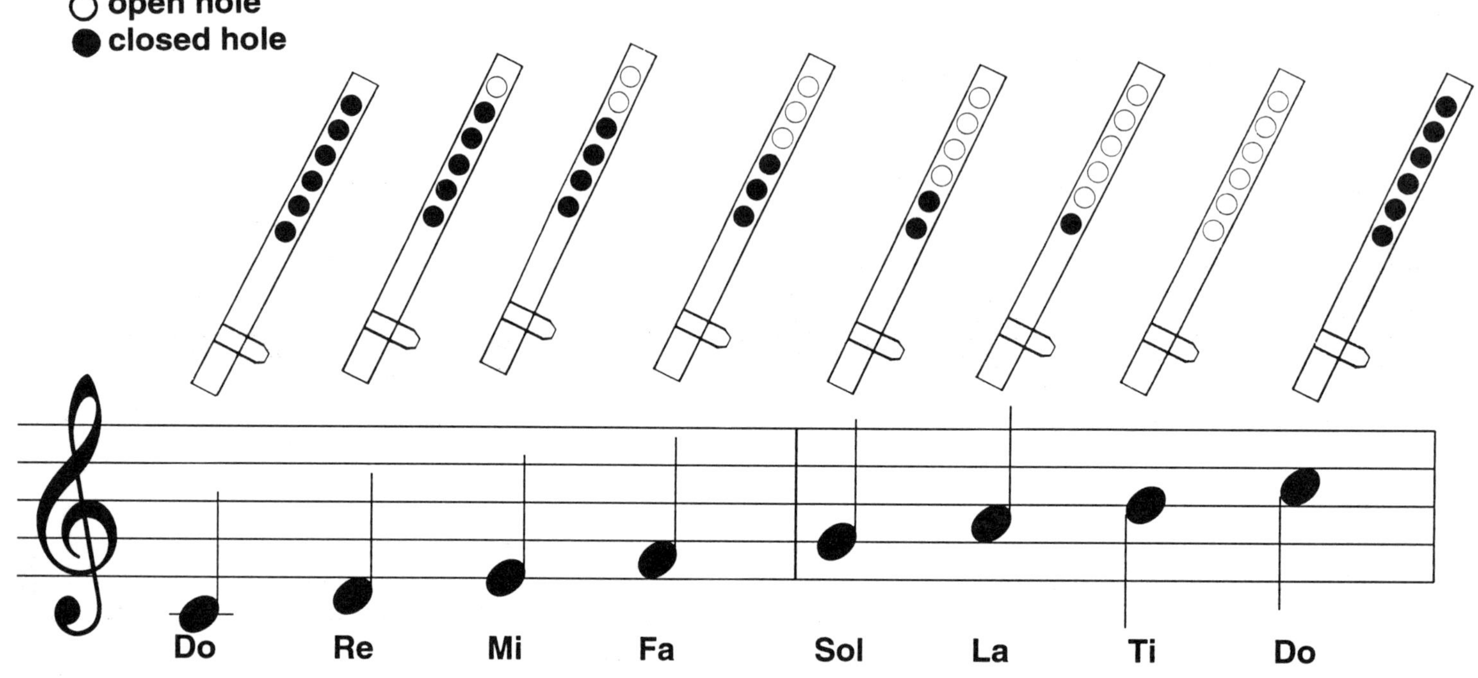

C Major Scale

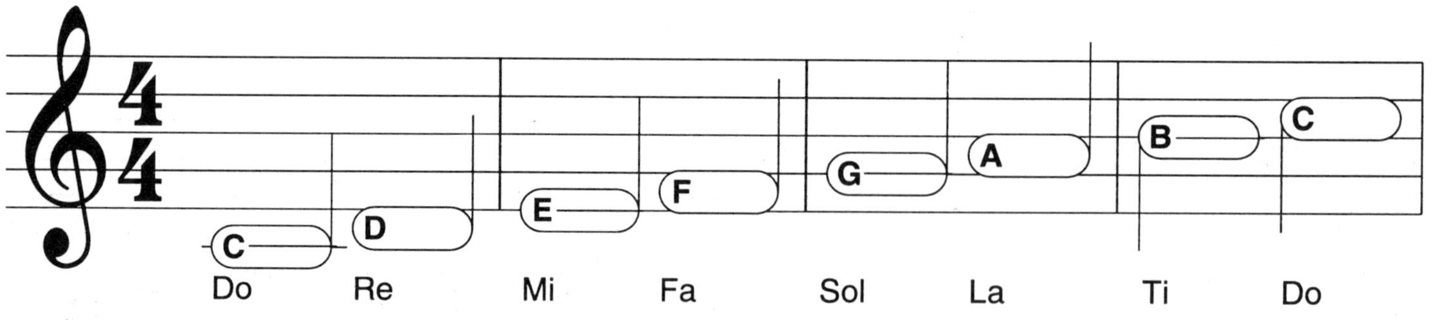

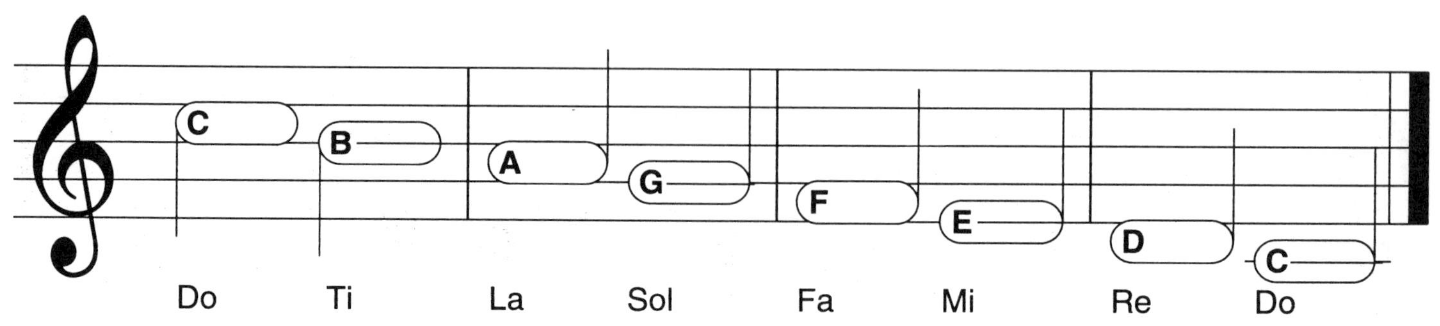

Theme by Beethoven

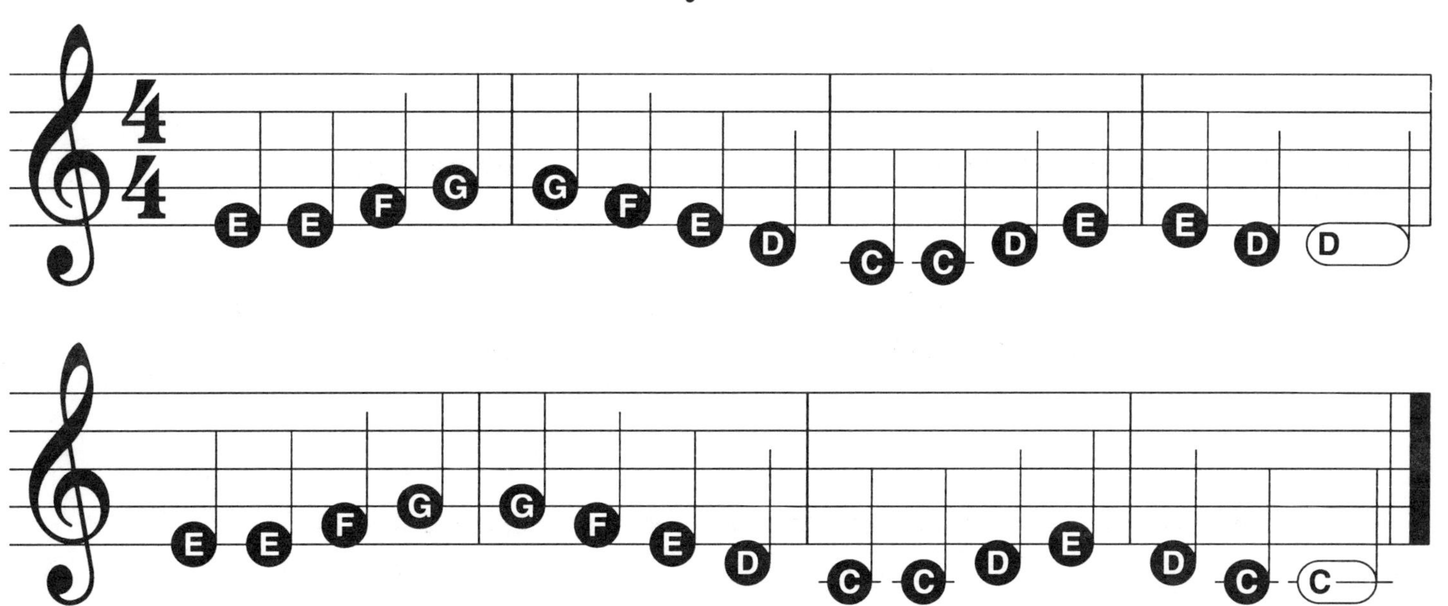

Go Tell Aunt Rhody

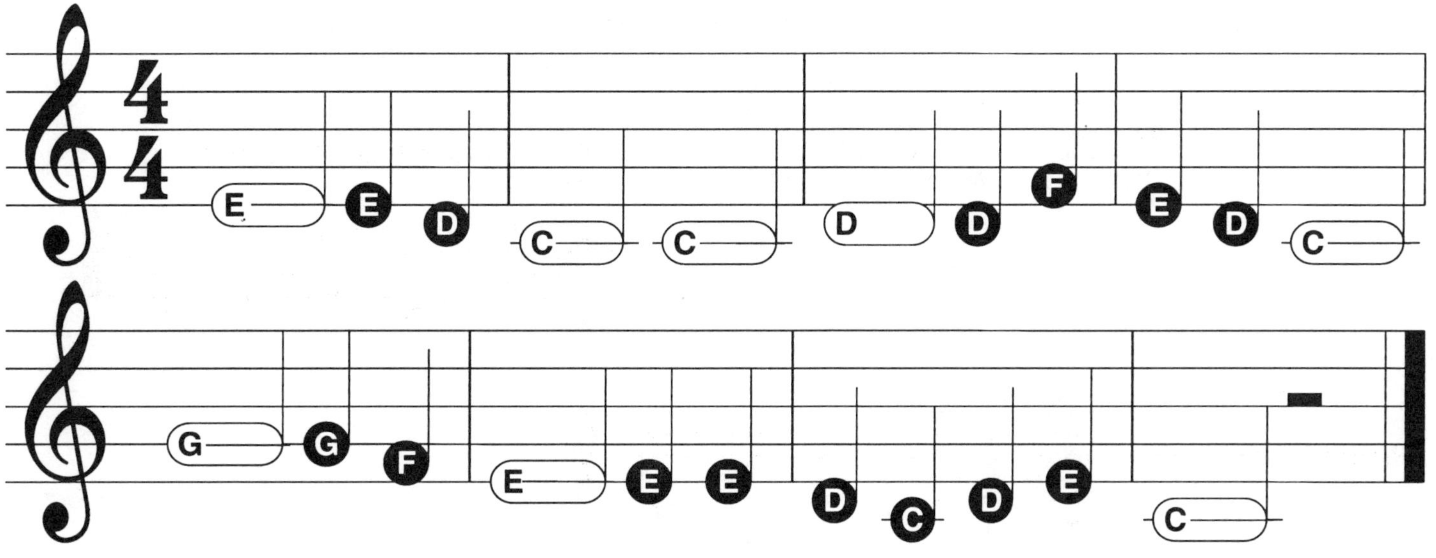

Lightly Row

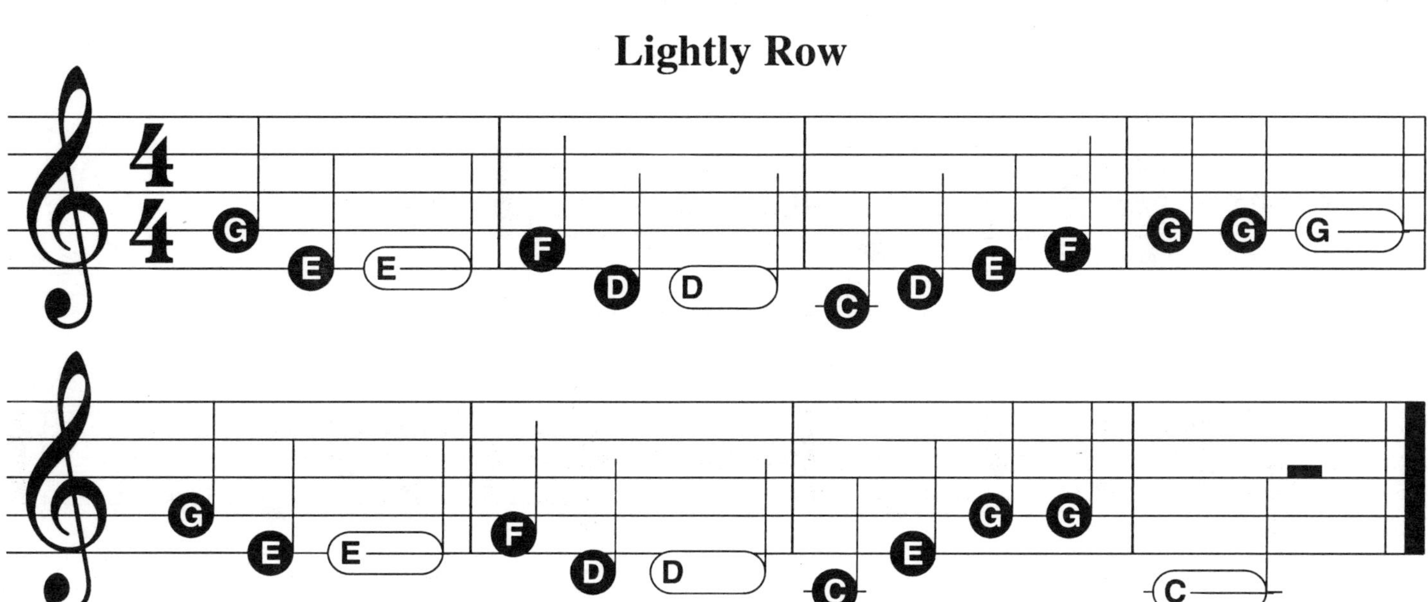

Note and Rest Values

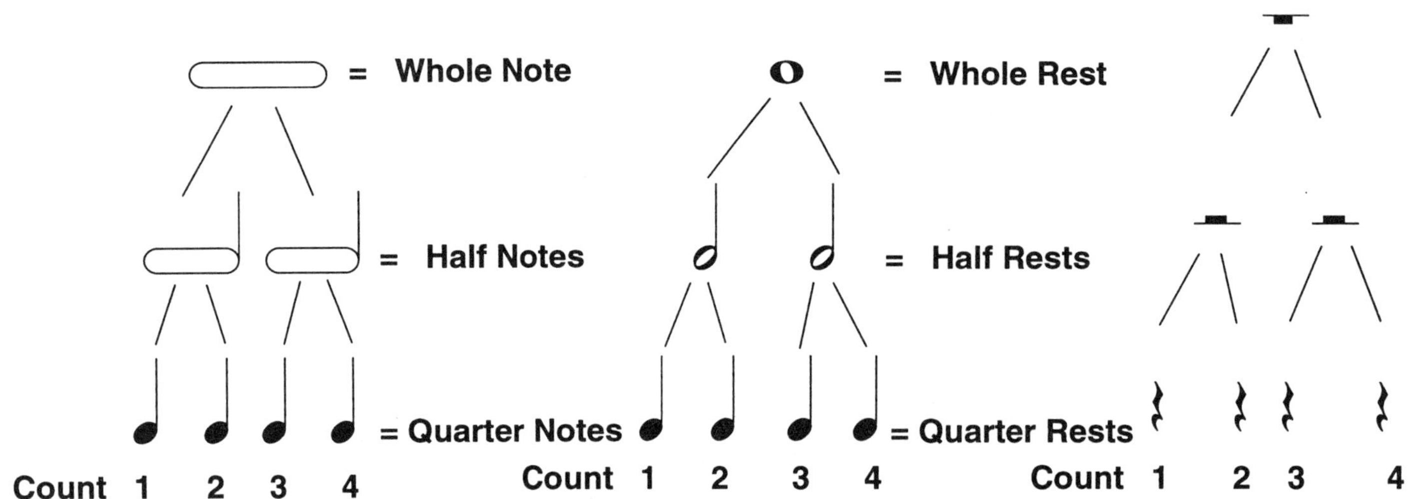

Note Reading

Fill in the names of the notes and play each word:

1. A hen's 

2. Do this every day! A good 

3. Happy Father's Day

4. An old 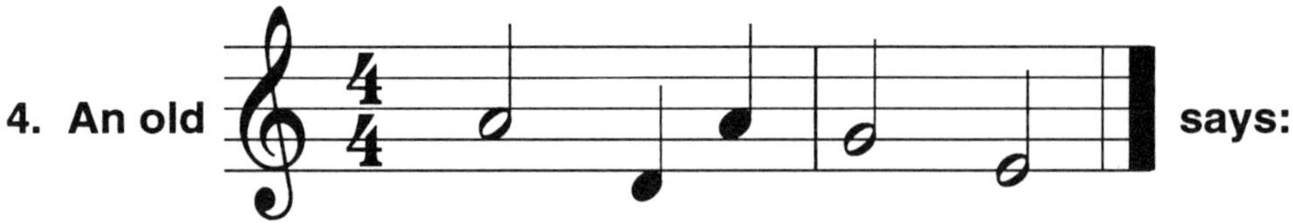 says:

A new 

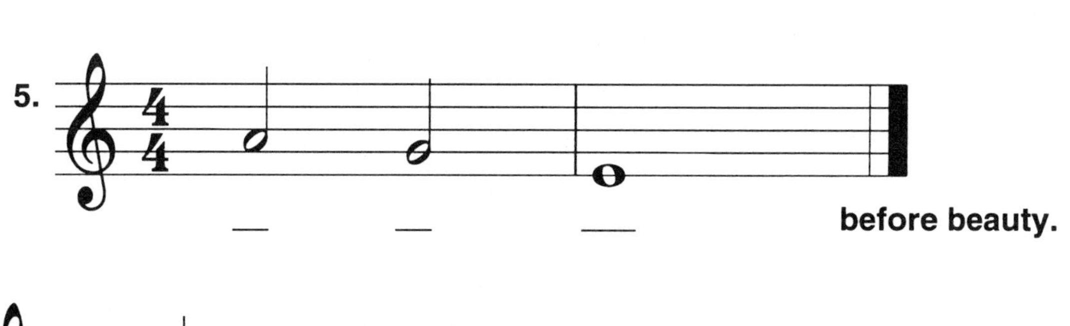

5.

before beauty.

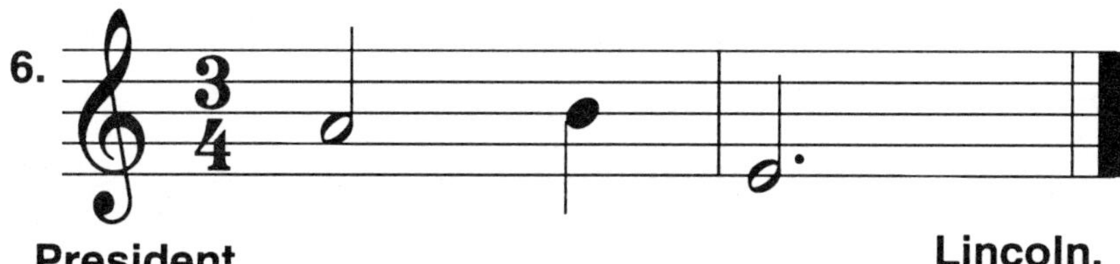

6.

President ___ ___ ___ Lincoln.

7.

___ ___ ___ of spades.

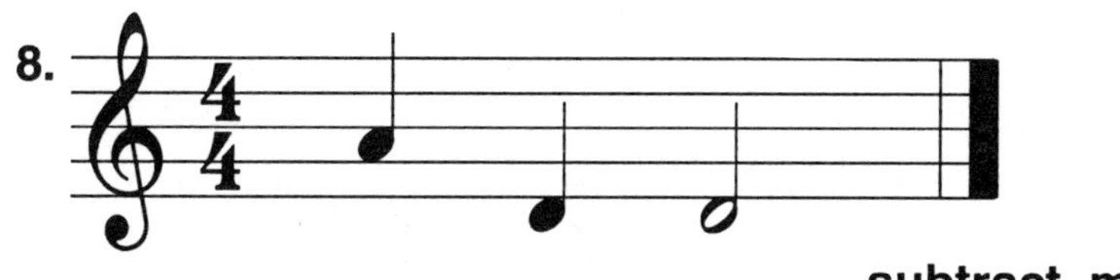

8.

___ ___ ___ subtract, multiply, and divide.

9.

Pick up your suitcase at the ___ ___ ___ ___ ___ ___ ___ claim.

10. Adding sweetness to your tea, With the work of the honey 

___ ___ ___

11. On the verge of a discovery, on the cutting 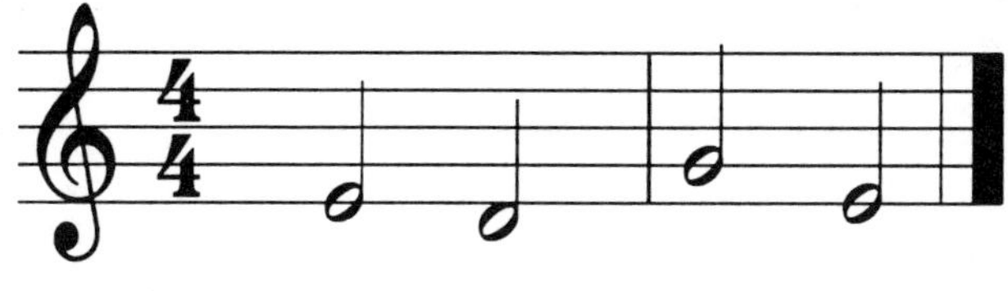

___ ___ ___ ___

12. The ocean tides ___ ___ ___ and flow.

Dotted Half Note

Count 1 2 3

Tie

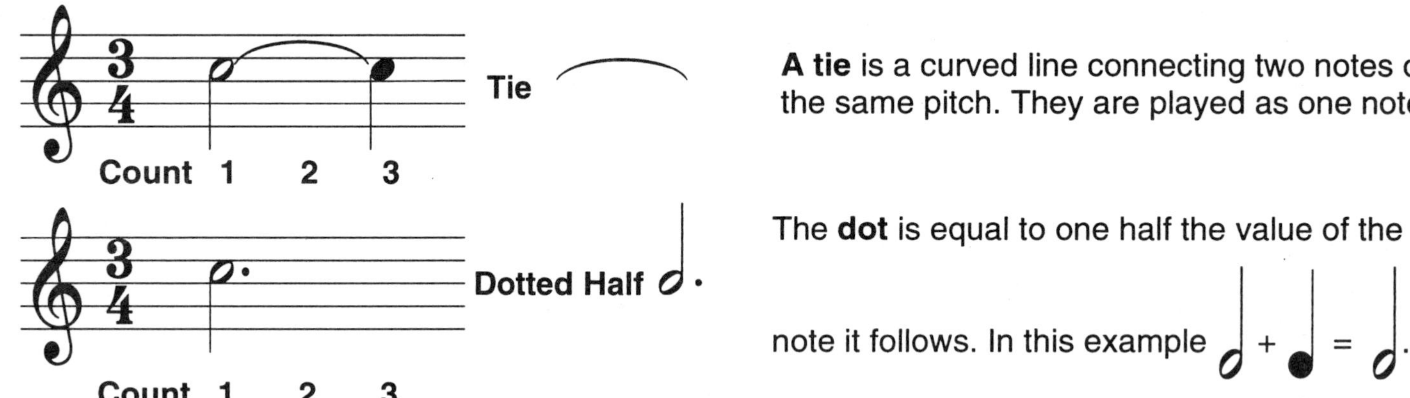

A tie is a curved line connecting two notes of the same pitch. They are played as one note.

Count 1 2 3

Dotted Half

The **dot** is equal to one half the value of the note it follows. In this example

Learning to Read Music

In order to read musical notation you must learn the names of the notes on the staff. Practice by writing note names beneath the staff.

Oats, Peas, Beans, and Barley Grow

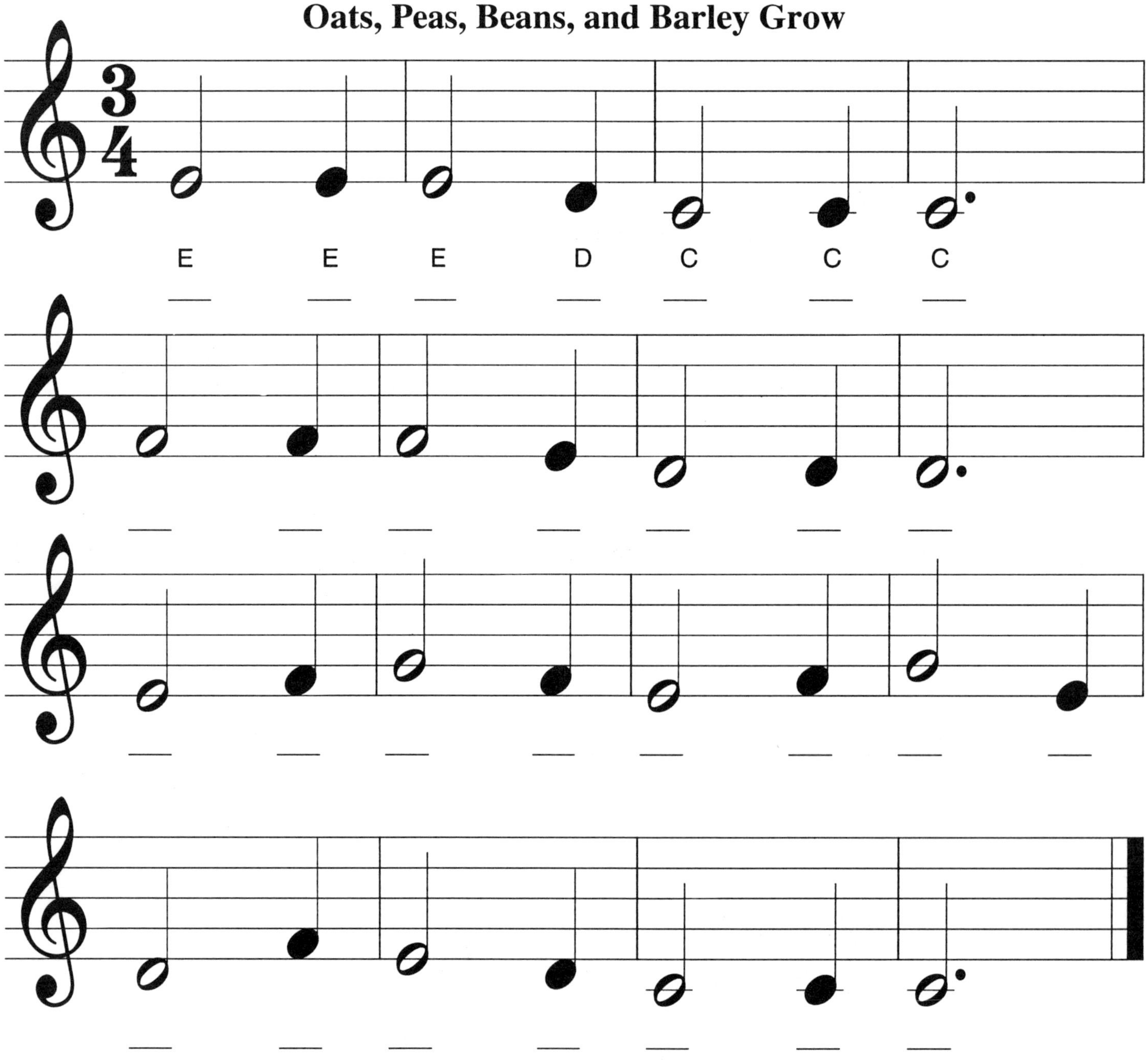

Round

A **round** is a piece in which two or more players begin at different intervals in the music. The following round can be played by two or three players. Each player begins when the previous player reaches the end of the first line.

O, How Lovely is the Evening

Chimes of London

Twinkle, Twinkle, Little Star

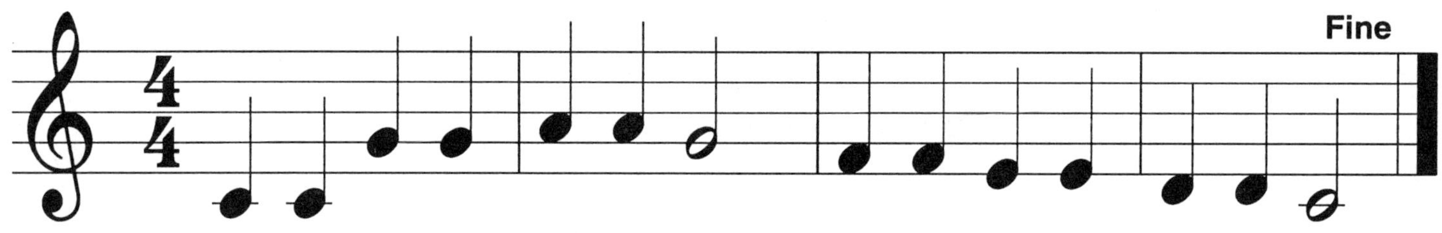

D. C. al Fine is an abbreviation for Da Capo al Fine.
D. C. al Fine means to repeat from the beginning to a place marked Fine.

Jolly Old St. Nicholas

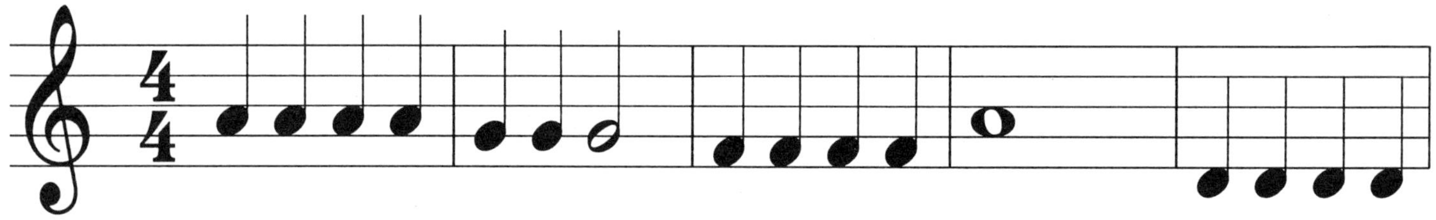

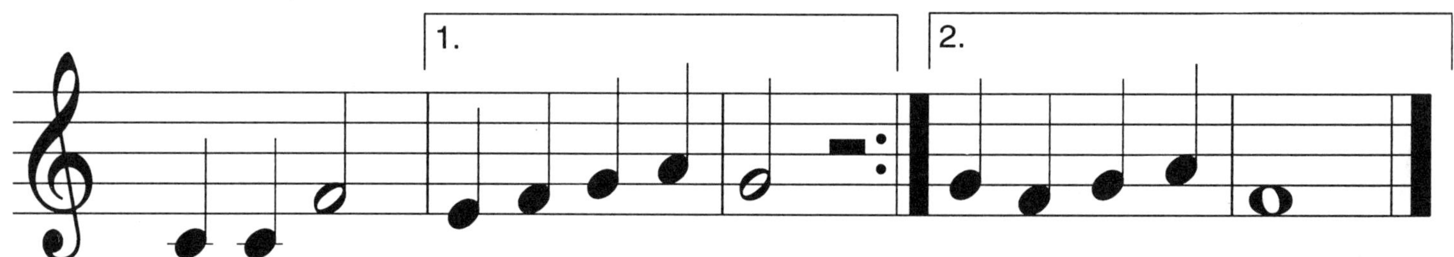

First and Second Endings

London Bridge

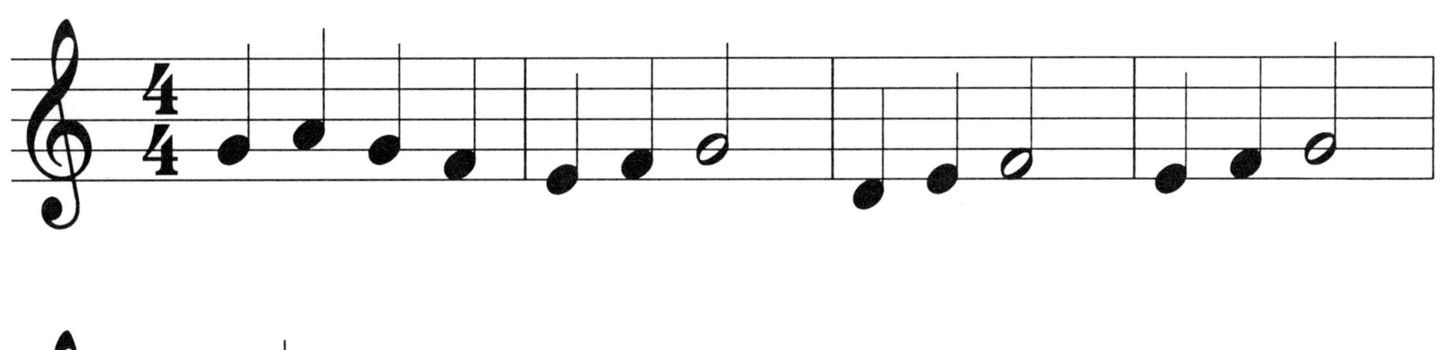

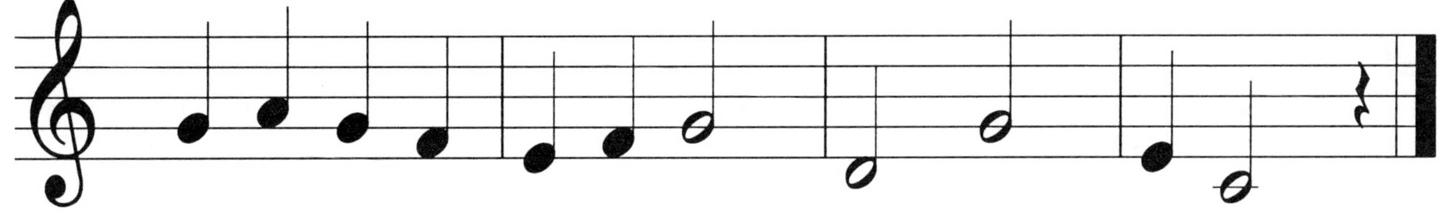

Over the River and Through the Woods

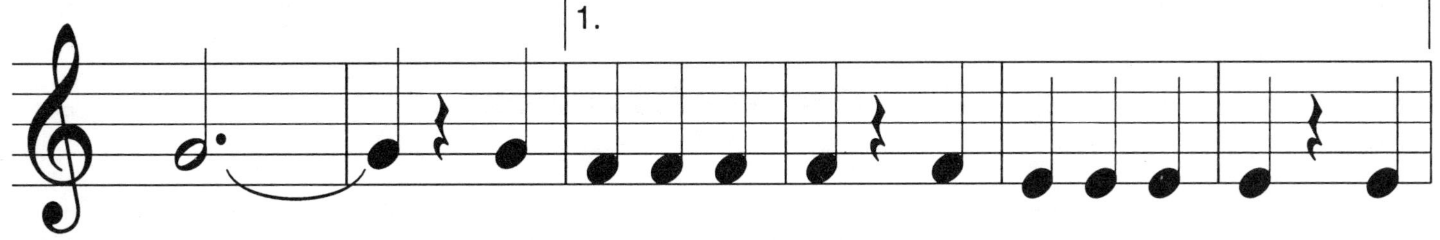

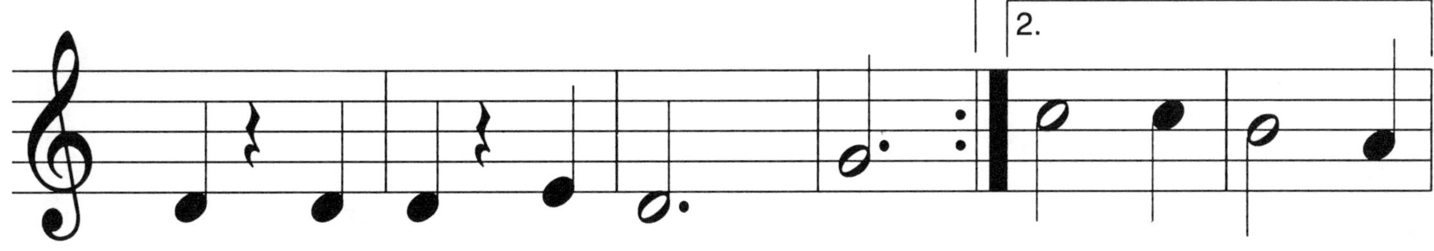

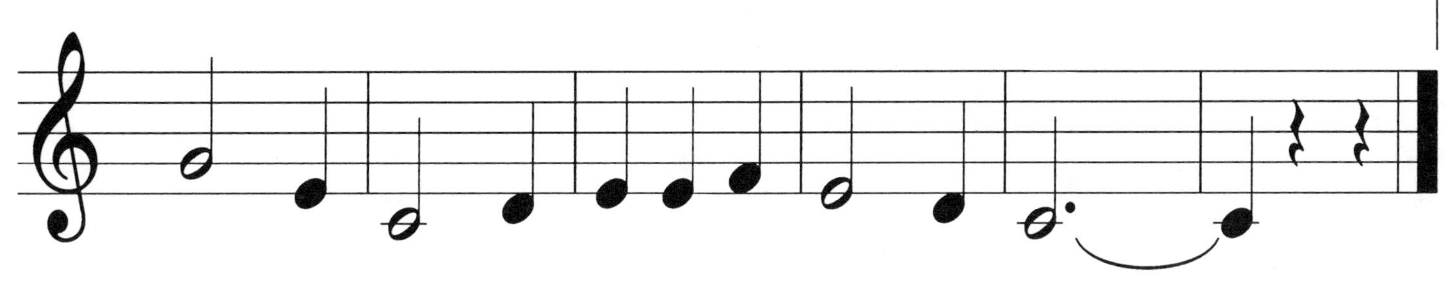

Three Blind Mice (Round)

Row, Row, Row Your Boat (Round)

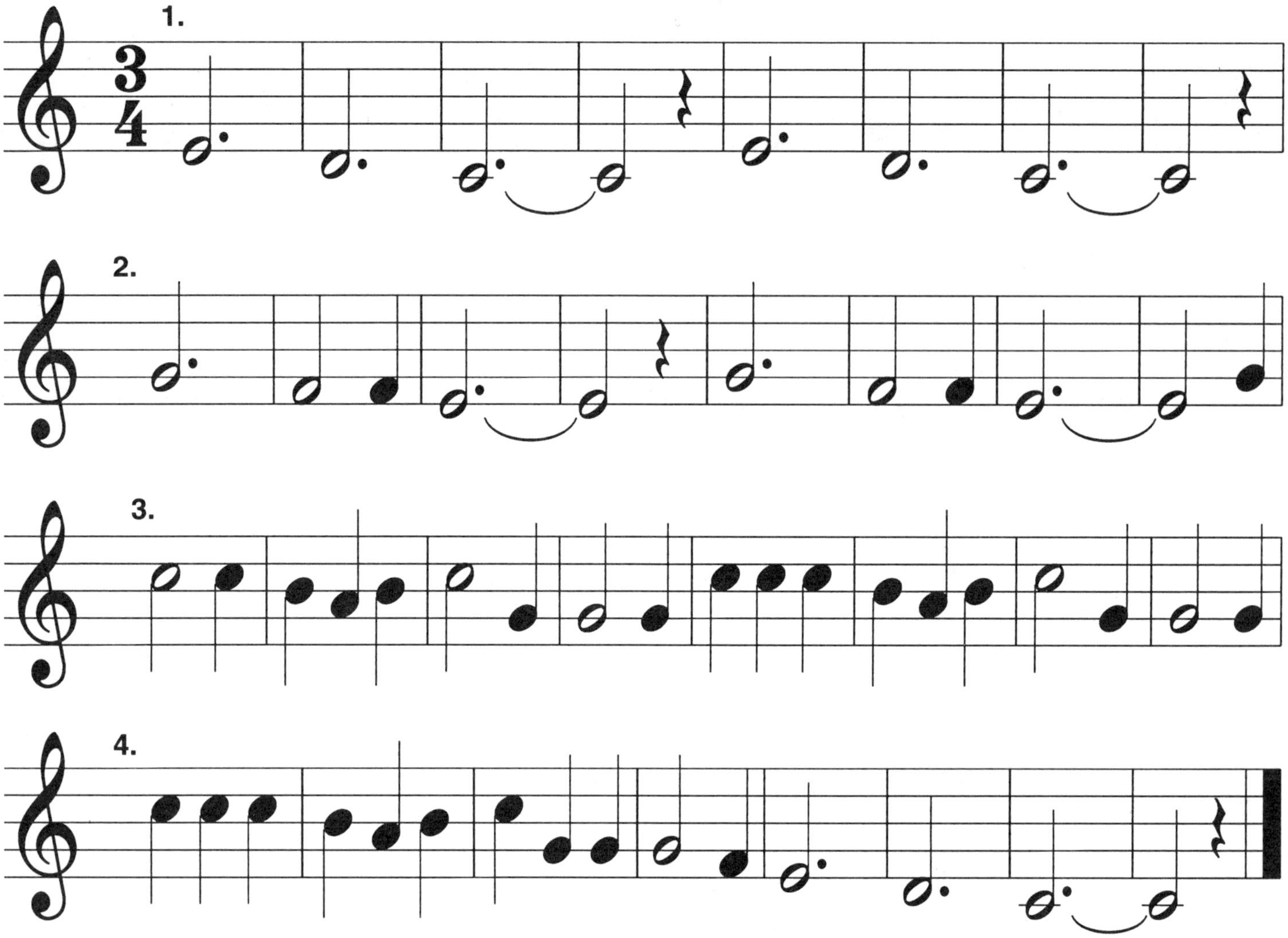

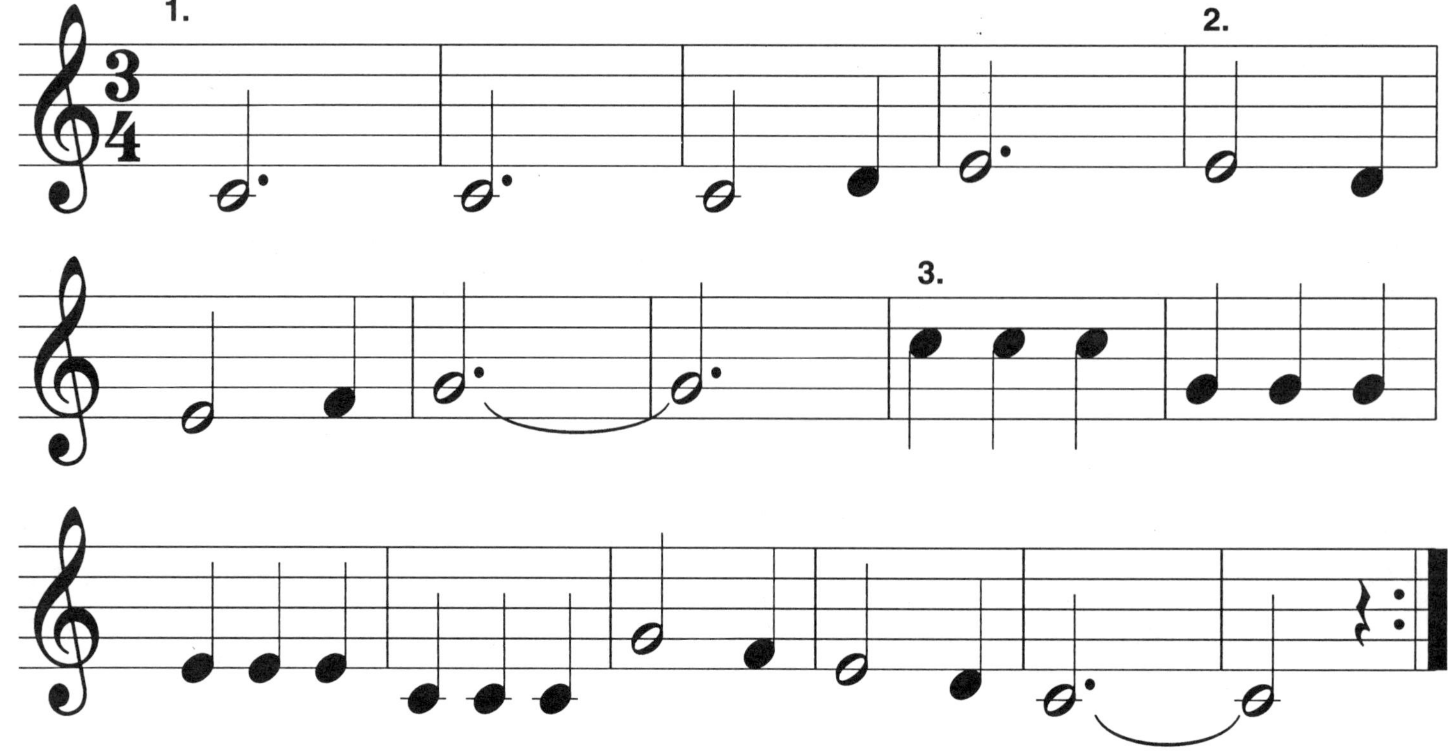

Pick-up Note

The following piece begins on the last count of the measure.
This note is called a pick-up note.

For He's A Jolly Good Fellow

Many pieces begin on the last count of a measure. The following piece, for example, begins on the last three counts in the measure. These notes are all called **pick-up notes.**

When the Saints Go Marching In

A Tisket A Tasket

Cindy

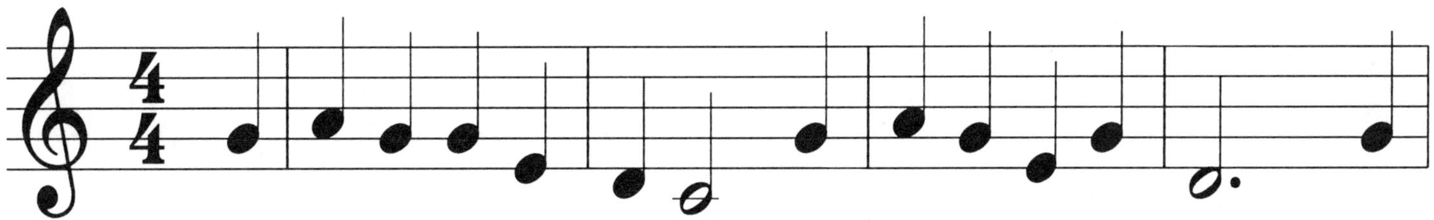

She'll be Comin' 'Round the Mountain

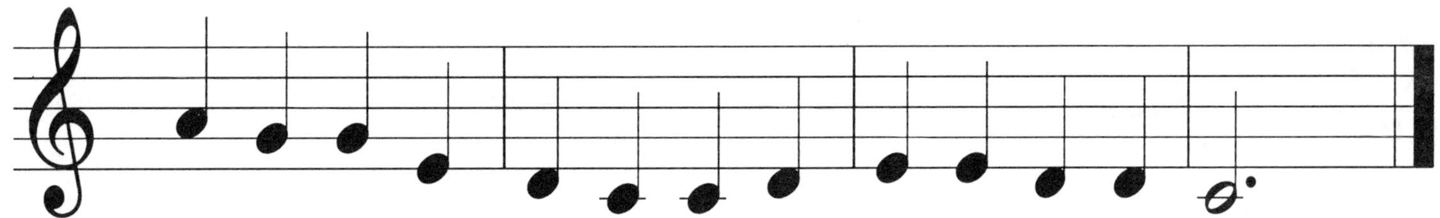

On Top of Old Smokey

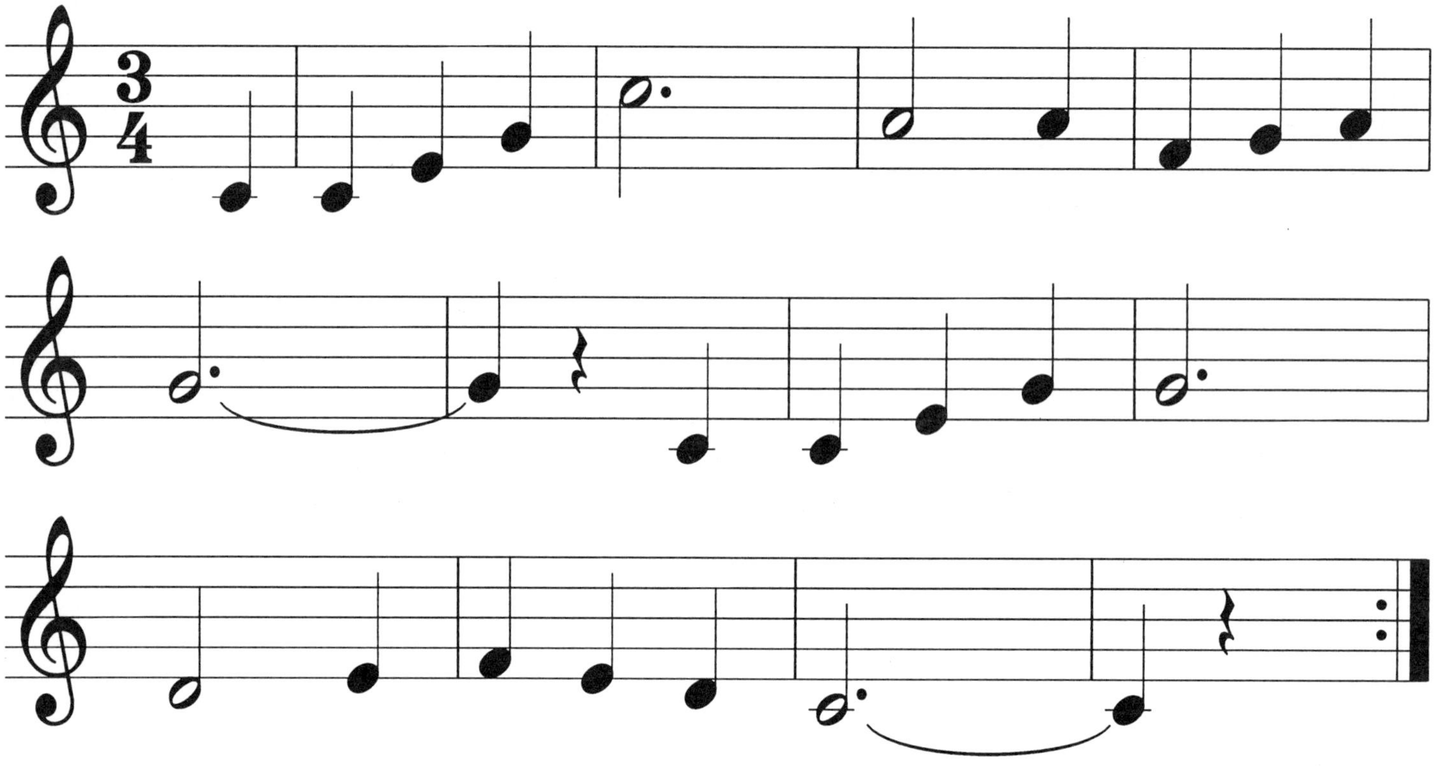

Blow the Man Down

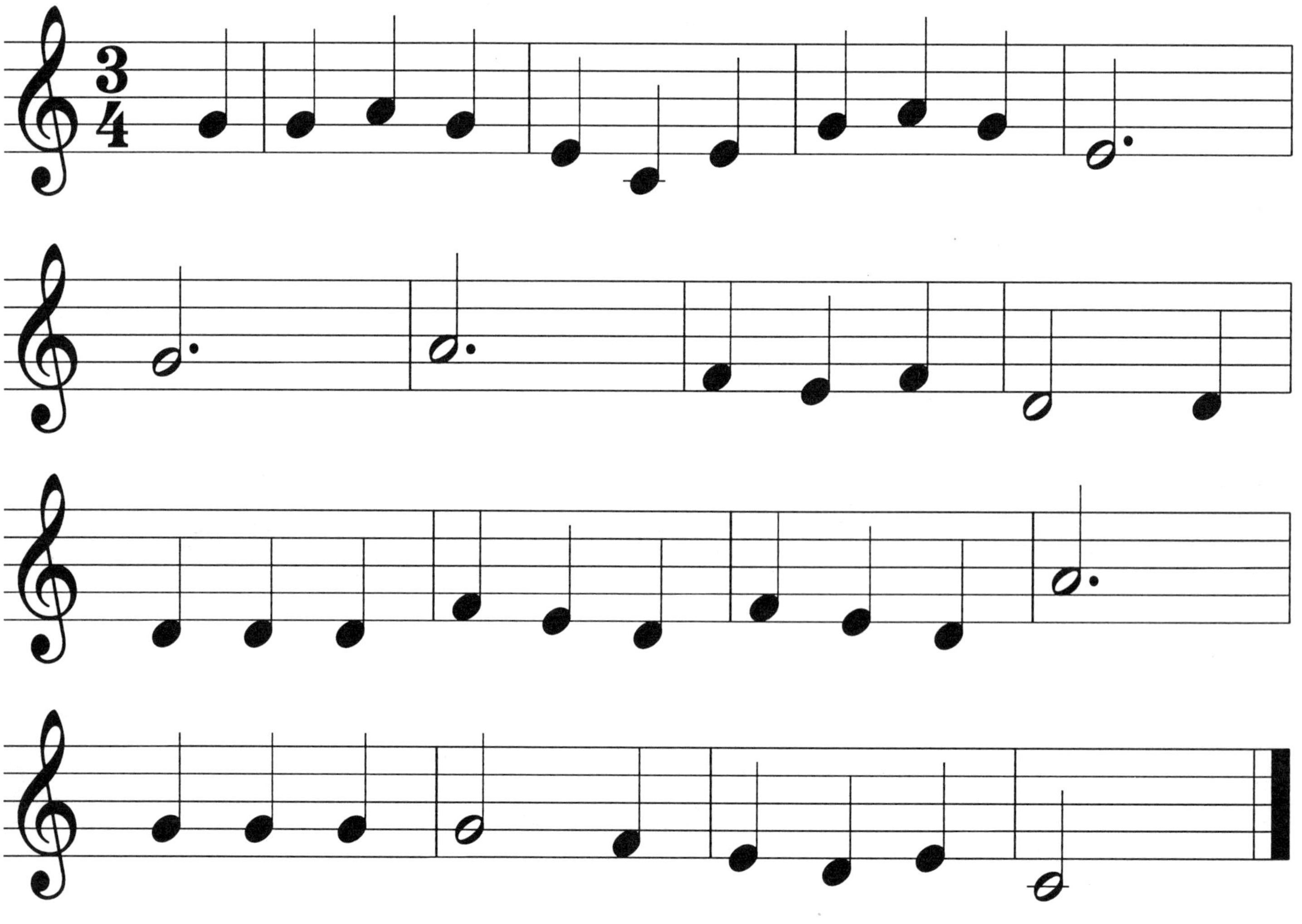

Eighth Notes

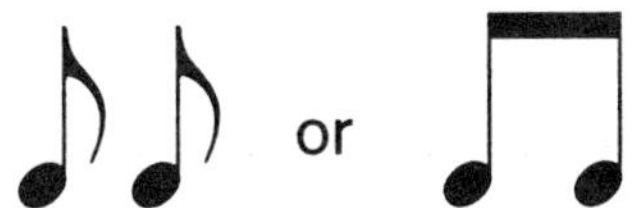

The **eighth note** receives one half of a count and is written with one flag or connecting bar.

Use the quarter note beat when counting eighth notes, and divide each beat into equal parts.

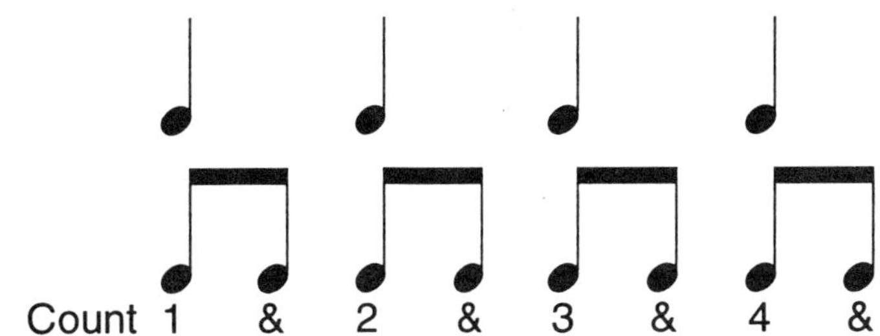

Eighth Note Exercise

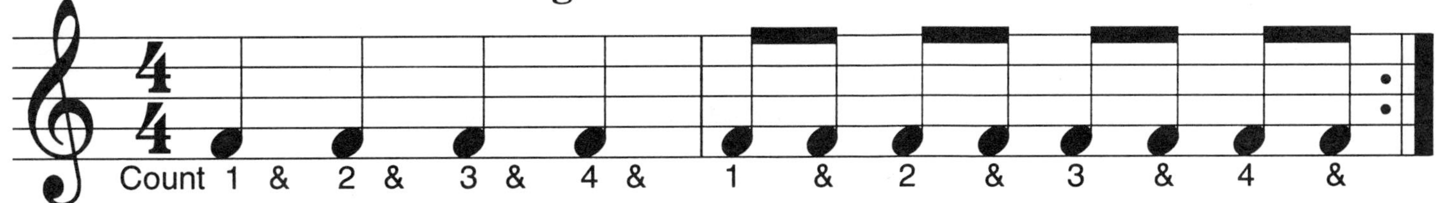

This Old Man

Jingle Bells

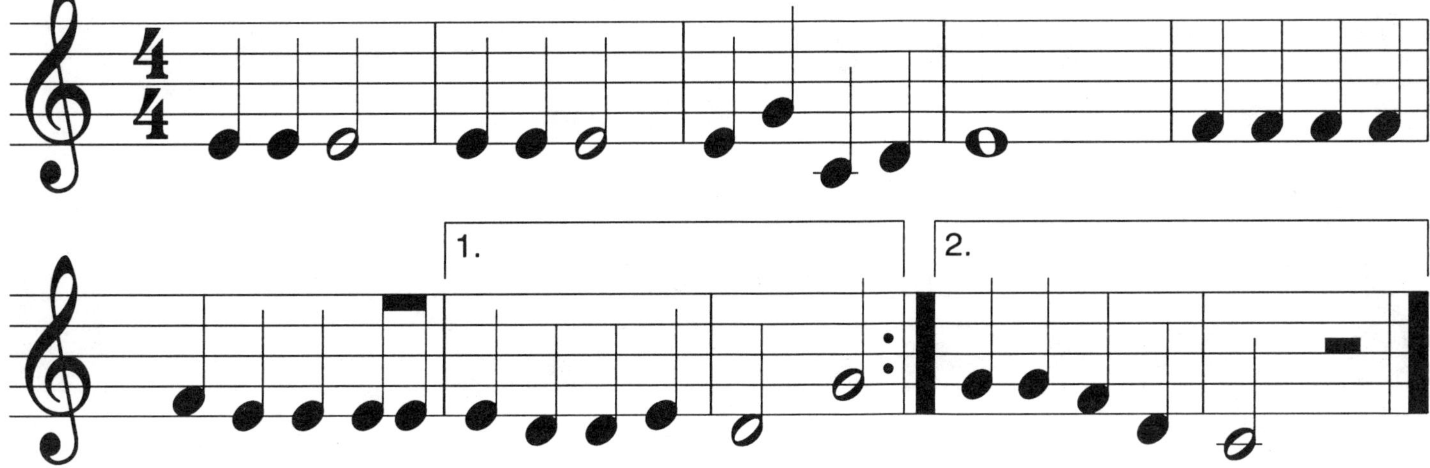

Long, Long Ago

Lavender's Blue

A Hunting We Will Go

Extended Fingering Chart

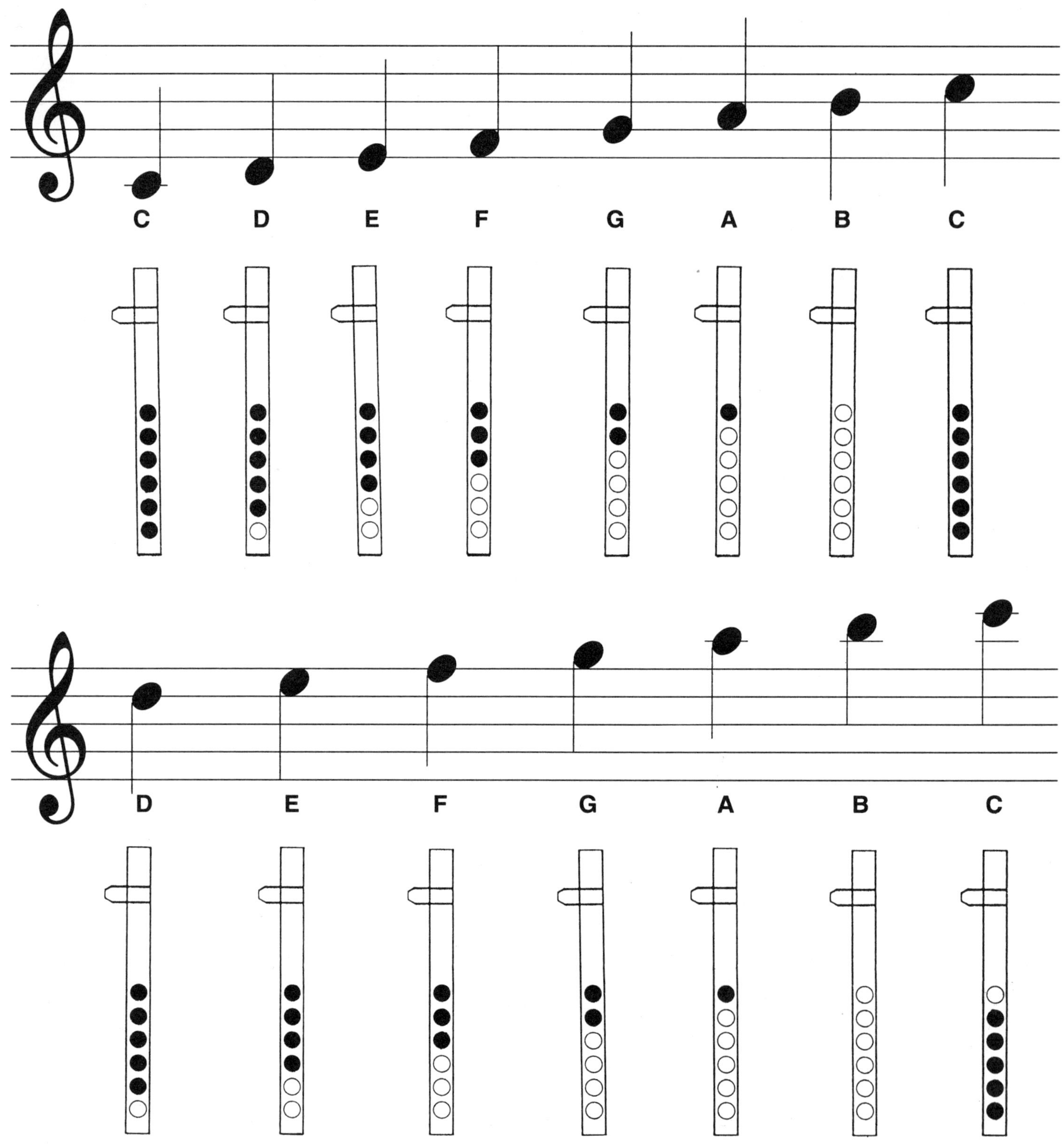